I Luv Myself

The mantra for SUCCESS...

A 365 Days Personalised Life Changing "I LUV MYSELF" Program for Families with Manukul

Would you like to have the opportunity to have MANUKUL as your personal Life Mentor/ Coach so that you can bring a change in your attitude, behaviour and performance in your daily activities which will bring the SUCCESS and enrichment that you want in your LIFE? 6TH Sens inc. offers an innovational life changing program for you and your family members for the first time.

Manukul will personally train and coach the parents as well as their wards throughout the year. This will bring a TOTAL paradigm shift in attitude, behaviour and performance through his personalised training and coaching methods.

HIGHLIGHTS

- MANUKUL will meet all family members at your home at least 12 days in a year and invest his 36 hours in 365 days.
- MANUKUL will communicate personally to each and every person of the family on alternate saturday or sunday on a prescribed scientific and psychological formats in follow up and continuous counseling program.

Note: MANUKUL will take only 30 families in a year.

To book MANUKUL as your family Mentor/ Coach / Trainer, email your request at 6thsensmail@gmail.com.

I Luv Myself

Manukul
A world-class Trainer & Motivational Speaker

PUSTAK MAHAL®

Published by

Pustak Mahal®, Delhi

J-3/16, Daryaganj, New Delhi-110002

☎ 23276539, 23272783, 23272784 • *Fax:* 011-23260518

E-mail: info@pustakmahal.com • *Website:* www.pustakmahal.com

Sales Centre

10-B, Netaji Subhash Marg, Daryaganj, New Delhi-110002

☎ 23268292, 23268293, 23279900 • *Fax:* 011-23280567

E-mail: rapidexdelhi@indiatimes.com

• Hind Pustak Bhawan

6686, Khari Baoli, Delhi-110006

☎ 23944314, 23911979

Branches

Bengaluru: ☎ 080-22234025 • *Telefax:* 080-22240209

E-mail: pustak@airtelmail.in • pustak@sancharnet.in

Mumbai: ☎ 022-22010941, 022-22053387

E-mail: rapidex@bom5.vsnl.net.in

Patna: ☎ 0612-3294193 • *Telefax:* 0612-2302719

E-mail: rapidexptn@rediffmail.com

Hyderabad: *Telefax:* 040-24737290

E-mail: pustakmahalhyd@yahoo.co.in

ISBN 978-81-223-1119-8

Edition : 2011

Printed at : Param Offsetters, Okhla, New Delhi-110020

Dedication

To my God Sri SAI Baba, Who loves me. I bow to His feet .He is ANTARYAMI. I always feel His Omnipresence. Without Him, I can't write even a single word, let alone writing a book. He is the writer within me.

To my loving mother Smt. Tripura Devi, who left this world for heavenly abode on November 15, 2009. She was, is and will remain the source of inspiration for me. She always wanted to see me successful and happy.

To my respected father Sri Ram Krishna Thakur, who always taught me discipline and values. He used to search only positive things in me. He never scolded and demotivated me in my teenage and adulthood. He was a freedom fighter, teacher, writer and philosopher.

And, finally to my guru Sri Sri Ravi Shankerji, who loves me. I bow to his feet. I always pay my gratitude and respect to him by performing *"Sudarshan Kriya"* daily.

To My Beloved Mother – Tripura !

Maa! You left this world for your heavenly abode on 15th Nov'09, leaving me orphan. It is 15th Nov'10 today and not a single day has gone by when I have not missed you in last 365 days. Maa! I know you were not happy with me. I could not live up with your expectations. Maa! you loved me through out your life. You sacrificed your life for me. But I could not love you. I always fooled you .

You were restless and anxious since 7th June'05, after the severe business loss. Maa! you always taught me values, discipline, courage, perseverance, honesty, kindness, time management, humbleness, renunciation, and service. You had shown me the way to understand the world better. I learned to dream BIG from you only. You taught me to live life on my conditions. Maa! why didn't you trust me?

Maa! I could not give you happiness and comfort when it was needed most. How much mental pain and agony did you bear in last few months of your life due to me, often, I think, feel and weep! Maa! please forgive me. I know that you are not alive now but, your spirit is and will always guide and bless me. I bow to your feet.

Maa! I LUV YOU, LUV YOU, LUV YOU. This one is for you, Maa!

Acknowledgements

I am very thankful to Mr. Ram Avtar Gupta, Chairman, **Pustak Mahal,** for taking his keen interest and proactive decisions in bringing out this book in its present form.

I can't forget to thank Mr. S.K. Roy, Mr. Zaheer Hasan and S.C. Bhati of Pustak Mahal for their support in designing and other support work.

In the end, I apologise for any inadvertent omissions and invite suggestions and comments for correction and rectification in future editions.

Contents

I LUV YOU

I luv the most positive and lovely teens/adults, who always inspired me to write this book by their day-to-day activities:

Archana, Manisha, Swati and Shruti	:	My Nieces
Ravi and Harsh	:	My Sons
Sameer, Nischay, Prem, Ayush & Piyush	:	My Nephews

I especially want to thank Archana, Manisha and Swati for changing my perception about myself and thus, changing the images in my subconscious mind. I really love you. You are my role models.

I cannot forget to say "I Luv You" to all the students who have attended my "I Luv Myself" workshops.

I THANK YOU

I am thankful to the most positive, committed and daring persons in my life, who kept believing in me in spite of all the sufferings. They have always motivated me to write this book. I can't think of my life without them:

Nirupma Khan	:	My mother-in-law
Anukul and Srikul	:	My elder and younger brothers
Praveen (Bablu)	:	My Nephew
Poonam	:	My Wife
Kanchan	:	My chief coordinator, who typed the manuscript.
Suresh Prasad	:	My friend and guide
Babulal	:	My friend and photographer

I am thankful to my brothers-in-law for their negative criticism and always doubting in my abilities which motivated me to write this book. I can't forget to thank my uncle and father-in-law for their help.

I cannot forget to thank the principals of all the schools who have given me the opportunity to conduct "I Luv Myself" workshop in their schools.

And finally, to all the people who worked with me sometime or the other (in my professional and business career) and their love, hate and ditch, which have made myself to start exploring ME!

My sincere thanks to each one of you.

I LUV MYSELF and YOU

MANUKUL

FOREWORD

After working with more than 60,000 students across India, while training them in my "I LUV MYSELF" workshops in public and government schools/colleges, I felt a need to write a book which would help the students of age group 12-20 years to change their perceptions about themselves.

Students in this age group are confused, restless and distracted because of TV, Internet and Mobile and are losing confidence in themselves. It is paramount responsibility of teachers and parents as well as students to understand the importance of perception, belief, self-affirmation, visualisation, role modelling and goal setting, suicidal and successful patterns and laws for students.

Students are losing their identity and they have created a false and wrong perception and belief about themselves and are ultimately failing. This leads to alcohol, drug abuse and psychosomatic diseases in students of this age group.

This book is written in such a manner that anybody can easily understand the awesome power of mind and mind power reprogramming processes to achieve success.

The title of this book is self-explanatory. "I LUV MYSELF" is the mantra for success.

So, start reading this book and improve your self image by chanting "I LUV MYSELF" within, all the time start verbalising, visualising and emotionalising your dreams and become a winner.

I LUV MYSELF and YOU

MANUKUL

CAUTION!

Students, as you are in your prime time developmental age between 12-18 years, you can build or ruin your entire life during these years.

You are exposed to TV, Internet and Mobile today and during these years hormonal changes are taking place in your system, too. If you are not programming your mind to be positive and goal oriented, you are programming your mind to be negative and this will lead to disappointment, frustration & failure.

You are always listening and watching negative messages from your surroundings, too. Please understand very clearly that you have to control your life by controlling your conscious thought patterns minute after minute and day after day. In the process of thinking, no one is going to help you. It is you, who has to programme your mind for success.

Every **Success** in life;

BIG or small, originates in your

MIND.

Goal focussed verbalisation and visualisation is the mental programme of a winner. You have to recreate the winning images of yourself which will lead you to realise the success in reality.

– MANUKUL

Every child is a born genius.

Out of 100 children, 90 are potential genius.

Parents, teachers, school, friends and society make them average and small in just 18-20 years.

Potential winners and greats are converted into average and small people by us.

Very few, who escape our pressures and tactics of making them small and average,

become successful and greats!

– MANUKUL

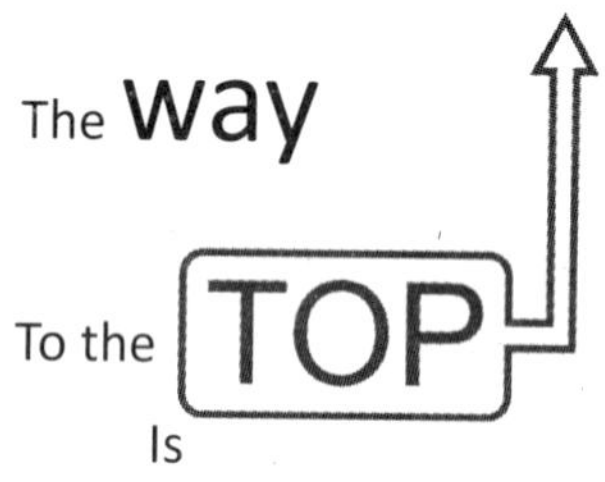

Easy for some and difficult for others,

But

Open to all!

– MANUKUL

I hold it true that **thoughts** are things,
They are endowed with bodies, breath and wings,
And that we send them forth to fill,
The world with good results or ill.
That which we call our secret thought,
Speeds forth to earth's remotest spot,
Leaving its blessings or its woes,
Like tracks behind it as it goes.

We build our future, **thought** by thought,
For good or ill, yet know it not.
Yet so the universe was wrought,
Thought is another name for fate;
Choose then thy destiny and wait,
For love brings love and hate brings hate.

– Henry van Dyke

Thoughts are the original source of all

Success, **prosperity**

and

happiness.

Thoughts are also the source of all failure,

poverty,

disappointments and *unhappiness.*

Thoughts

are electrochemical impulses.

Thoughts are Magnetic in nature and thoughts have a frequency too.

Around 60,000 Thoughts enter into our mind during 24 hours.

Thinking is the highest form of activity a person is capable of doing, yet very few really **think!**

Thinking is the hardest work, this is the reason why so few **engage** in it.

– Henry Ford

Do you know, you actually think about **images**

and not in **words?**

Don't you remember, your mom taught you 'A' for Apple, 'B' for Ball, when you were just 3 years old?

You learned 'A' when you saw 'Apple'.

Isn't it?

You think either positive or negative.

(+) Positive means creative and constructive.

(-) Negative means despairing and destructive.

Positive thinking leads to progress and prosperity.

Negative thinking leads to retreat and

defeat.

As you think, those Thoughts

are sent out in to the entire UNIVERSE

and they magnetically attract all **"Like Thoughts"** that are roaming and floating in the UNIVERSE on the same frequency.

So, if you are Thinking Negative, all Negative Thoughts roaming in the UNIVERSE will rush to you to make

you fail and bring unhappiness, disappointment and frustration!

But, if you are Thinking Positive, all Positive Thoughts roaming in the UNIVERSE will rush to you to make you successful and happy!

Every **thought**

has an "idea" or verbal component,

an "image" or visual component and

an "emotional" or feeling component.

– James Newman

You think in three-dimensional format, i.e.

verbal, visual and emotional.

Your body is made up of five basic ELEMENTS :

Earth

Water

Air

Space

&

Fire

and so is

UNIVERSE.

You have **five** senses, through which information is collected.

They are **sight**

sound

smell

taste

&

touch.

(Eye, Ear, Nose, Tongue, & Skin)

6th
Sense

The sensory perception, the intuitive power, the inner voice

It is the only thing that matters

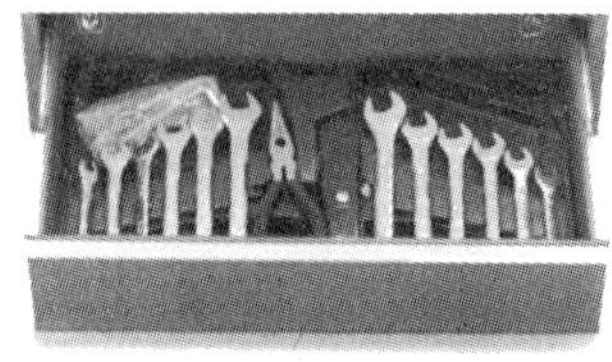

EQUIPMENT

Figure it out for yourself, my lad,
You have all that the greatest of men have had,
Two arms, two hands, two legs, two eyes,
And a brain to use if you would be wise.
With this equipment they all began,
Do start from the top and say, "I CAN"

– Edgar Guest

DEVELOPMENTAL AGES and INFLUENCING FACTORS

1-7 years	:	Mother
8-12 years	:	Parents, Friends and TV
13-21 years	:	Role Models, friends, TV, Internet and Mobile
21 onwards	:	Marriage, family, self and profession

See the change in your Thinking, Feeling & Doing patterns as you grow: My Papa, When I was ?

4 Years young	:	My Papa can do anything.
5 Years young	:	My Papa knows every thing.
6 Years young	:	My papa is smarter than your's.
8 years Young	:	My Papa doesn't know every thing.
12 Years Young	:	My Papa doesn't know any thing . He is a fool.
16 Years Young	:	Don't pay attention to my Papa. He is an old fashioned and outdated man.
20 Years Young	:	My Papa is hopeless.
25 years Young	:	My Papa knows a little bit.
35 Years Young	:	Shall I ask my Papa what he thinks. After all he is experienced.
40 Years Young	:	I always talk to my Papa first before doing anything.
45 Years Young	:	I wonder how Papa would have handled. He was so wise and Had a world of experience.
50 Years Young	:	I am too bad. I had never appreciated my Papa. I could have Learned a lot. Sorry Papa, I missed you all the time.

BIOLOGICAL CHANGES

Hormonal changes start taking place in you from the age of 12 years. With these changes, you start **thinking, feeling** and **behaving** differently.

You are not a kid now. You are now entering into your life.

The life ahead is not easy. This is the reason God is giving you the required necessary strength through hormones, so that you can win the struggles of life!

You are receiving Testosterone and Progesterone.

(Testosterone, a male and Progesterone, a female hormone)

The process of **growing up** from childhood to adulthood can be very

trying and frustrating.

You undergo rapid physical and emotional changes during this age, i.e 12-18 years.

In girls, the breasts begin to develop, the hips widen, and hair begins to grow in the pubic area and under the arms. Menstrual cycle starts.

In boys, the penis, testicles and scrotum develop, shoulders broaden, and hair begins to grow in the pubic area, under the arms and on the face. The voice deepens. Emission of semen also begin.

You will become a complete **man**

or a **woman** by the age of 18.

You should be

thankful to GOD

that HE has trusted you.

There are many "TRANSGENDERS" on this planet. They are neither

male nor female.

Think and thank

your God with gratitude.

Mind – the master equipment

The human brain is the most complex biological structure known to exist on the earth.

It has been estimated by experts that it would take 10 million years to count the number of nerve connections in the brain.

Mind is a

Goal Seeking Machine.

Mind is 'The Modem of Universe'.

That means, Mind works as Transmitter of

UNIVERSE;

(The Ultimate or Supreme Mind.)

Mind is a HUMAN TRANSMISSION TOWER and this tower

is the most powerful transmission tower in the

Universe.

Human Mind

is always connected to

the **Universal Mind** with

'THOUGHTS'

and Human Mind

can be controlled by

'BREATHE'.

The Universal Mind

The Universal Mind is not only
INFINITE intelligence,
but it is substance and this substance is the attractive force which brings ELECTRONS together by the law of ATTRACTION so they form ATOMS; the ATOMS in turn are brought together by the same law and form MOLECULES; MOLECULES take objective forms and so we find that the law of attraction is the creative force behind every MANIFESTATIONS, not only of atoms, but of world, of the Universe, of everything of which the imagination can form any conception.

— Charles Haanel.

To become conscious of this power is
to become a "Live Wire".

This Universe is the Live Wire.

It carries power sufficient to meet every
situation in the life of every individual.

When the individual mind touches the Universal mind,
it receives all it's POWER.

— Charles Haanel.

Mind weighs only about 50 ounces in male and 45 ounces in female.

It requires **1/10 volt** of electricity to perform efficiently. This electricity is generated by thoughts. So, we can't live without thinking. The moment we stop thinking, we are dead.

It contains 100 billion neurons, which work as files.

Mind has three compartments:

Conscious mind

Subconscious mind

and

Super Conscious mind

The end part of mind structure is called Brain Stem, which is merged with spinal cord. Mind + spinal cord is known as

Central Nervous System (CNS).

Whatever mind thinks and decides consciously, spinal cord passes the decision to every part of the entire system for action.

The Conscious and Subconscious mind play totally different roles, yet they play their roles in complete harmony.

The cerebrospinal or voluntary system
is the organ of the conscious Mind.
The autonomic or involuntary system is the organ of
the subconscious Mind.

The voluntary nervous system is the channel through which your Conscious Mind receives all the data through your sense organs which creates PERCEPTION. And, exercises voluntary control over the movement of your BODY. This system has it's control panel in the CEREBRAL CORTEX of the Mind.

The autonomic or involuntary nervous system has it's centre of activity in the other part of the Mind, including the cerebellum, the brain stem and the amygdale. These organs of brain have their connections with the major systems of the body and support their vital functions even when conscious awareness is absent, i.e while sleeping.

While you are asleep, your heart continues to beat rhythmically, your chest and diaphragm muscles pump air in and out of your lungs. Your digestive systems function on it's own through this autonomic system.

The **conscious mind** is around 10% of total mind power.

Its role is to collect the information through five senses from the outside world, compare it with previous experiences, determine the relevance and then finally make a decision in

yes or no.

The **subconscious** mind is around 90% of the total **mind power.**

It is a large data bank. It stores all the data which is accepted by the **conscious** mind..

Over 90% of your life is

Subconsciously programmed and governed.

The **subconscious** mind is like computer files.

What you have decided consciously,

gets registered in your subconscious

mind in three-dimensional format.

It is like an **obedient servant.**

It can't reject the decisions and orders of a **conscious mind.**

Subconscious Mind

is like *"Alladin's Giene"*.

Whatever decided and accepted by the Conscious Mind knowingly or unknowingly, positive or negative, the Subconscious Mind – The Jinn, accepts the decision as it is in the form of IMAGES with feelings and connects with the Universal Mind for the realisation of the IMAGES into REALITY.

So, if you want to achieve your Dream, just ask your *"Giene"* and you will be given. But remember one thing very clearly that this *"Giene"* understands the language of IMAGES only, not words.

You always walk, talk, think, feel, behave and perform in a manner consistent with the subconscious images and these images are programmed by your conscious decisions that you have made minute after minute and day after day.

If you see it in your Mind,
you are going to hold it in your hand.
So, it is rightly said,

"Thoughts are Things."

Think Good and, Good follows.
Think Bad and Evil and, the same will come to you.

Your *"Giene"*, i.e Subconscious Mind

doesn't argue with you. If you say, "I am poor and

can't afford it, "your *"Giene"* sends the message
to the Super Conscious Mind which releases the
news to the Universal Mind and all poor making
forces roaming and floating in Universe on the same
frequency rush towards you with
a great speed to make you

POOR.

So, you are what you **consciously** decide for yourself and keep telling all the time in your conscious mind.

If you keep your conscious mind **focussed on what you want** rather than what you don't and keep on telling all the time in your mind, you will become **what you want in life!**

Here is the real problem.

Most of the people around 87%

are always busy in thinking about what they don't want.

It is because they are always distracted and

deceived by their EYES.

As per one report, Conscious Mind receives around 87% data through EYES, 9.5% through NOSE, TONGUE & SKIN and, only 3.5% through EARS from the outer world.

This is the main reason of distraction during the age12-18 years.

So, listen to your EARS, not your EYES.

Your EYES create false PERCEPTION especially during this age.

"Naino ki mat suniyo re, Naino ki mat maniyo,
Naina Thag lenge!"

So, watch what you think, feel and do.

Never say *"I am poor, I will fail , I will loose my job, I can't score good marks , I can't get success."*

Think, Speak, Focus and Act on

what you "want" only.

You can be successful when you take control of your thoughts entering into your conscious mind from minute to minute and day-to-day.

You should be thankful to your God
that there is a time delay in conversion of your

"Thoughts" into "Things"!

This time delay serves you and helps you to reassess and change your thinking patterns about what you want and to recreate new picture images, because your God always wants to make you

SUCCESSFUL & HAPPY.

Mohandas Karamchand Gandhi, an **ordinary** advocate, was thrown out from the train on a chilly winter night in South Africa. He started **thinking** differently and **rediscovered himself** and today he is known as

BAPU or THE FATHER OF THE NATION.

Isaac Newton also did the same serious **thinking** when he witnessed an apple falling and discovered the law of gravity.

Today he is known as

Sir Isaac Newton.

So, conscious and abstract thinking made them GREATS

Barack H. Obama	:	The President of the United States of America
Nelson Mandela	:	The President of South Africa
Bill Gates	:	The founder of Microsoft Inc.
Abraham Lincoln	:	The great President of the United States of America
Sachin Tendulkar	:	The legendry cricketer
Akshay Kumar	:	Successful Bollywood star
Amitabh Bachchan	:	The superstar of Bollywood
Dhirubhai Ambani	:	The Father of Industrial Revolution in India
Henry Ford	:	The Successful Carmaker.

What about you:

....

With the mind you possess, you too have the potential to become successful!

To become **successful,**

you have to think differently and abstractly.

Animals don't think **abstractly.**

"Bhains ke agye bin bajayee,
Bhains rahee pagurayee!"

Can you convert FIVE into FOUR?

Your life is not mathematics, which moves by some fixed patterns like a mathematical formula – $(a+b)^2 = a^2+b^2+2ab$.

From the age of 12 onwards, you have to start removing bad habits and weaknesses and enhance your skills to get success.

(You have to erase F and E to get roman iv)

So, every problem you are facing today is an opportunity in disguise. You just see **differently** and you will get surprises. Never make judgment in hurry. This prejudgment about

THINGS, PEOPLE & CIRCUMSTANCES

is the basic reason of

FAILURE!

From the age 12 onwards, you have to start removing bad habits and weaknesses and start adding skills in you after doing proper **SWORD** analysis to become

successful.

SWORD

Identify and Analyse what you have :

S	:	STRENGTH
W	:	WEAKNESS
O	:	OPPORTUNITY
R	:	RESOURCES
D	:	DREAMS

Sit comfortably with a pen and paper. And start enquiring and putting questions to yourself to identify your SWORD:

- What is my natural strength? Which are the subjects I enjoy while studying? Which are the areas I am strong at?
- What are my weaknesses and shortcomings?
- What are the opportunities I have today and will have in future, in my area of interest?
- What are the resources I have in my hand today? My family background, my school, my friends, etc.
- What is the purpose of my life? What are my dreams?

Always use **W7H**

To get the right answer from **yourself!**

(W7H : what, when, where, who, which, whom, why and how)

"W7" is under your control but,
"H" is under the control of your

GOD.

So, always use W7 to yourself!

- Who am I?
- Where am I?
- What do I want?
- What are my strengths?
- Where do I want to go?
- To whom shall I meet & talk?
- What should I do to achieve my dreams?

Never think "HOW" would I achieve my DREAMS?

Perception is what you see through your

mind, not by your sense organs.

If the data, information received by the conscious mind is incorrect then the perception will also be incorrect. This is the reason, sometimes you perceive rope as a snake.

TRUTH

Are you sitting in your study room? Your are wrong!

You are rotating and moving towards East at the speed of 1000 mile per hour. As the earth is moving around the sun, you are moving in another direction at the speed of 2000 mile per hour and as the sun is rotating in a Milky Way Galaxy, you are flying away at the speed of 15000 mile per hour.

All these directions are realities.

(These all are mataphysical data.)

So, don't you think

your perception that you were sitting in your study room was wrong

because your input was wrong and incorrect as it was collected by your eyes.

How can you say that you can't become **successful**

in spite of your present conditions and circumstances!

This speed was felt and utilized in positive direction by Lord Buddha, Mahatma Gandhi, Nelson Mandela, Mother Teresa, Einstein, Bill Gates, Amitabh Bachchan, Sachin Tendulker, Dhiru Bhai Ambani, Abraham Lincoln, Barak Obama, APJ Abdul Kalam and all successful people!

I had also felt this speed, when I lost everything on 7th June'05. This speed was working against me as I was afraid and always expecting some bad news and I kept on receiving all bad news. I lost my business. The moment I received this news, I started thinking about what would happen next with fear and anxiety. *Things, events and circumstances* unfolded on me with a great speed with all negativity. I lost my properties. I lost my savings. I lost my cars. I lost my house. I lost my parental property and I lost my beloved mother too. She could not bear the pain of these severe losses. I lost my all self-esteem and image and in the same continued speed; I reached New Delhi in search of life and livelihood. Here, I got some quiet and peaceful moments. I started thinking differently. I used W7H. I again took my SWORD (Strength, Weakness, Opportunity, Resources and Dream) analysis. I purchased around 200 books in one day. I started dreaming again. I kept all my problems aside. I recollected all my positive energy. I came to Shirdi and prayed to my SAI and

I got the answer.

I started training and motivating students, parents and teachers, what I learned from my life. I was surprised by this speed again. But, this time speed was working in positive direction. I conducted around 100 "I LUV MYSELF" MPR workshops/seminars across India and abroad in just 365 days. All my problems started diluting on its own.

I restored my self-esteem and image. I started regaining my lost confidence. This simply proves that to achieve BIG you just make a BIG dream or purpose for your life and visualise the end results all the time and you would be surprised by the speed. Your weight of your dream and your speed will create a MOMENTUM and everything required to make you successful will start happening automatically and you will start flying.

$$M \times V = \text{MOMENTUM}$$

M= Mass
V= Velocity

The weight of your Dream x Speed = Smooth Takeoff.
BIGGER THE DREAM, SMOOTHER THE TAKEOFF.

But you have to remember one thing very clearly that if you are thinking negative all the time about yourself, your circumstances and your conditions, this speed will create a negative momentum and aura. This will start working against you to make you fail and bring disappointment, frustration and poverty. If this momentum is not checked in time by changing the thought pattern, this momentum will force you in a circle where you may loose your life. But, if you are thinking positive and having a BIG DREAM for your life, this speed will create a positive momentum and aura around you which will carry you through to your

DREAM and DESTINY.

RATNAKAR, the notorious dacoit converted himself to Maharishi Balmiki, a saint and wrote "THE RAMAYANA" in Sanskrit.

This is the live example of SPEED and MOMENTUM.

Balmiki started chanting – *MARA, MARA, MARA* with speed and he got RAMA, RAMA, RAMA – The Ultimate Destiny.

If you say MARA .... MARA.......... MARA............. MARA,

you will die.
Because, you lack SPEED.

But, if you say *MARA, MARA, MARA, MARA* .... With speed, you will get

RAMA, RAMA, RAMA!

This simply means if you don't have a BIG DREAM in your life, this Universal speed will work against you and make you FAIL. But, if you have a BIG DREAM, this speed will give you wings to fly and will bring flying colours of SUCCESS in your life irrespective of your present condition.

Another angle of this *MARA...... MARA....... MARA........* and RAMA...... RAMA........ RAMA concept is that the difference between DEATH (MARA) and LIFE (RAMA), FAILURE (MARA) and SUCCESS (RAMA) is your MOMENTUM only. For smooth takeoff, you must have very BIG DREAM for yourself.

By this concept Nelson Mandela achieved his purpose in life. The same way Barak Obama became the President of America. The same technique Dhirubhai Ambani, Amitabh Bachchan, Bill Gates, Akshay Kumar and many used to become SUCCESSFUL.

They not only worked very hard but also utilised the speed very smartly. They never committed the mistake of thinking and dreaming small. Their dreams were very BIG, so they took off smoothly. They suffered a lot in the process of their success journey. They faced many trials but they never stopped their journey. They kept on moving because of the positive MOMENTUM and they reached their destination. They realised their DREAMS.

False Data

Leads to

False perception

Leads to

False belief

Leads to

FAILURE!

What you see

Through your mind?

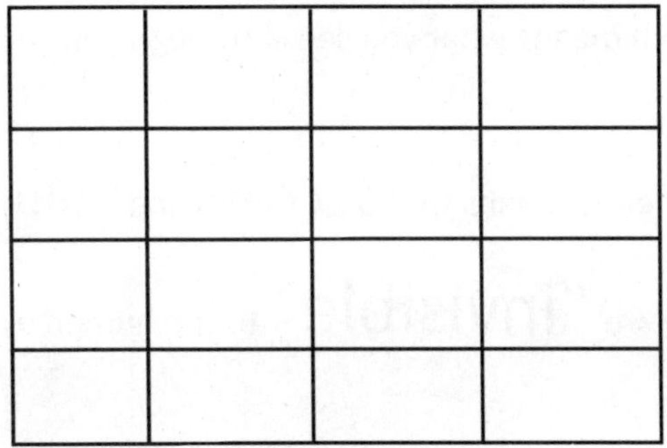

Some will see 16 squares. Some will see 26 and some 30 squares. It depends on your own perception which means what you see is through your mind.

This clearly means that success and failure in life are "invisible" to the human eye!

You don't know **anything** accurately

What you will become in **life**!

But

You have created false and wrong perception about

YOURSELF!

It is our duty as **men and women** to proceed as though limits to our abilities **don't exist.**

– Pierre Teilhard De Chardin

You are **empowered** to create your own reality by creating your own winning or failing **images** in your subconscious mind.

"3% of the population earns 97% of all the wealth on this earth. This is not an accident. Every one who has taken birth on this earth as a human being has potential to become RICH & POWERFUL. All are empowered for richness but only 3% THINK, FEEL, DO.....& SUCCEED in becoming RICH &

Creating or recreating mental images is called

Mind Power Reprogramming.

This simply means, you have to change your

average / negative **images** with successful / positive

images in your subconscious mind by
three-dimensional format

Verbalisation

Visualisation

and

Emotionalisation

Have you ever thought how you breathe,

how blood circulates

and food digests in your system?

These **life**-supporting activities are

subconsciously programmed

By

God

for your survival!

Your Subconscious, i.e. *"The Giene"*, is the builder of your body and maintains all it's vital functions. It works 24 hours and never sleeps.

Subconscious Mind is the COO (Chief Operating Officer), which operates entire operation of our system effectively, efficiently and enthusiastically and reports back to the chairman, i.e. GOD (Super Conscious Mind).

Can you believe the **awesome** power you have within the confines of your **mind?**

How much do you work to perform the following activities?

- You breathe 23000-24000 times, inhaling and exhaling 435–440 cubic ft of air in every 24 hours.
- Your heart beats 2 ½ billion times in 70 years.
- Your blood travels 6 lakh miles while circulating 1450 times to all capillaries in 24 hours.

Is it not Amazing?

This is your power.

Subconscious power!

Your *"Giene"*, i.e. Subconscious Mind speaks to you through intuitions, impulses, intimations, urges and ideas. The urge to love, to save the life of others comes from your Subconscious Mind.

The voice of *"The Giene"* is called

6th Sense

So

If you think, you are beaten, you are

If you think, you dare not, you don't

If you would like to win, but think you can't

It's almost certain, you won't.

If you think you will lose, you have already lost.

Success and failure begin with the

individual will and it is in the **mind!**

So

Change your

thinking ....

To change your

DESTINY!

To **exist** is

To **change,**

To change is to **mature,**

To mature is to go on,

Creating oneself endlessly.

– Henry Bergson

When you make changes in your thinking

You change your perception about yourself.

When you change your perceptions

You change your personal beliefs.

When you change your personal beliefs

You change your expectations from yourself.

When you change your expectations

You change your attitude.

When you change your attitude

You change your behaviour.

When you change your behaviour

You change your performance.

When you change your performance

You change your destiny and life!

This change comes when you Reprogramme your

Mind - The Goal Seeking Machine,

you possess.

Mind Power Reprogramming

Requires

Identification of your change areas!

I have worked with more than 60,000 students across India and identified that today's students and youths are facing

identity crisis.

Today's youths are not loving themselves!

But

loving someone else and suffering

from

'Luv'eria!

(Infatuation)

A false Perception

Thus

Suffering from poor-self-image problem.

I have heard one beautiful story from my English teacher when I was studying in Udai Pratap College, Varanasi. We, students and teachers of the college, used to call him "KAVI JEE". He loved me like his son. I used to spend my weekends with him. He was the disciple of OSHO. Today, he is not alive. I would like to pay my gratitude to him with this story which has immense value and meaning.

There was one boy, aged 16 years, decided to commit suicide by taking a jump from the roof of his 13th floor house. He was not happy and not enjoying his life. SO, he thought to end his life. One old man saw him jumping from 13th floor of that building. So, shouted loudly, "What are you doing my son? you should think about your parents before ending your life. you should love your parents. They are old and they have some expectations from you. They have worked hard in making you. They love you, my son!" "Nobody loves me and I don't love anybody" replied that young boy. The old man persuaded further and said, "Son, please think about your girl friend at least. Hope, you would love her. For that love, son, please come down." He shouted back on old man, "I don't have any girlfriend. I hate girls." Now, that old man prayed him and said, "Son, your life is precious. Love yourself. Don't kill yourself, son! You don't know who you are!" The young boy started laughing and replied, "Yes, I don't know who I am? If I knew this fact, why would I have thought to kill myself? I don't love myself."

Today, almost entire youth world is like this only. Nobody loves himself. Everybody is busy in loving others. How can you love somebody else, if you don't have love within you for yourself. If you have something in you, then only you can give that thing to others. If you have money, then you can help others with that money. If you have happiness, kindness in you then only you can spread happiness and joy to others. Isn't it? If you don't love yourself, how can you say "I LUV YOU" to others? If you say this "I LUV YOU" to others then you are fooling others. This is fact. Think and start loving yourself first before declaring your love to others.

Demonstration of your love towards others especially to your opposite sex during 12-18 years of age has become a fashion today. You have learned this fashion by watching films and television. This is not real love. This is deceit. This is a drama. This is acting. This is a false perception. Getting attraction towards opposite sex is very natural. You please don't get confused between "likings" and "love". You are receiving power hormones from 12 years onwards in your system. These hormones are creative hormones, sex arousal hormones. You start feeling attraction and sensuality towards opposite sex. Animals too feel this sex and sensuality. This is your creative strength and power. As you have a "master equipment" in the shape of your "Mind", you become supreme powerful. But, today the entire youth world around 87% are behaving like animals. Because you always think about sex like

animals do. I request you to hold this power and use in creativity like a human being. Think abstractly, behave like a human being, not like an animal. Your God is not happy within because He has created you different from animals. He expects from you to become a human being at least. So love yourself first before declaring it to others. Don't demonstrate your false love to your opposite sex like animals.

You believe it or not, 87%-90% of conflicts, mental diseases, suicides on this earth are because of these "I LUV YOU" bacteria. The early you understand and feel this creative power within, you will become SUCCESSFUL and POWERFUL. You are born as Xerox copy of your GOD. You are the "the image" of your GOD. Tulsidas had rightly said 1000 years back, "Jaki rahi Bhavana (Feeling) jaisee, Prabhu murat dekhi tin taisee."

WHERE IS YOUR GOD?

I would like to share with you one very important fact what I learned in my life. I 100% agree what OSHO had said many years back in his book "SEX TO GOD" and, VIVEKANANDA had said many - many years back . OSHO had clearly told the entire humanity to enquire your GOD within and you would find this GODLY POWER in centre of your BODY. This centre is under your genital/ sex organ. This power is called "KUNDALINI". This power has to travel towards your " MIND". OSHO says, "If this power always travels down wards, you will start behaving like animals. And, this happens when you always think about opposite sex, declare your love towards opposite sex." This means, if you always sit,

gossip, roam, party with your opposite sex, your "KUNDALINI", "GODLY POWER" will travel downwards, towards your feet. You will become restless, anxious, depressed, frustrated, angry and weak. you can't focus and concentrate. You can't sit even ten minutes at one place. You will feel insecured. You will always keep yourself busy in searching help. But, the moment you start loving yourself, this "KUNDALINI", "CREATIVE POWER" or "GODLY POWER" starts traveling up wards towards your MIND and you will start traveling towards your SUCCESS. This "KUNDALINI" or "GODLY POWER" or "CREATIVE POWER" can be directed towards Mind with your "BREATHE". you have to control your "BREATHE" to control your "MIND".

As, I said to you very early in this book that "MIND" is a Goal seeking machine, put one BIG goal, dream, purpose in this machine. Make your "images" how would you look and feel, when you accomplish your dream? Always see that image while sitting, walking, eating, travelling with your closed or open eyes. Within 21 days you will feel, you are a changed person. This change is the glimpse of that "GOD POWER" — that will appear on your face, in your walk and talk and in your style. if you keep focusing on yourself, loving yourself, your dream and your GOD, this "KUNDALINI" will keep on travelling towards your Mind and a day will come when you would have achieved success and you would have become a role model, super star, super successful person, social worker, an honest politician, a research scholar and saint, i.e the image of GOD. Health, wealth and the prosperity will follow automatically.

You don’t have to work hard to achieve anything. Everything will come to you automatically. This is MAGIC, CHARISMA. Start loving yourself and feel this magic, THE MAGIC OF GOD.

But, if this “KUNDALINI”, “Creative Power” travels downwards, you will start feeling “The MAGIC OF DOG”. You will behave like a DOG. You will start barking like a Dog, fighting like a DOG, demonstrating your love on roads like Dogs. And, your doggy activities will lead you towards Hospital or Jail! Even you may loose your precious life.

Awake! Awake! Awake!

and change yourself during these prime years.

Six most important change areas
For
Students/youth

- I want to **love** myself.
- I want to **enjoy** studies.
- I want to be **confident and focussed.**
- I want to be **fit and fine.**
- I want to **take control of my life.**
- I want to be a doctor, engineer, teacher, IAS officer (or whatever you want to be).

(Apart from the above-mentioned change areas, you may identify your own change areas where you want to improve but always remember, these six change areas are the key areas where every student has to change to get success.)

Corresponding self affirmations with winning picture images :

Change Area	:	I want to love myself.
Image	:	I see myself handsome or beautiful.
Self Affirmation	:	I love myself
Change Area	:	I want to enjoy studies / my work.
Image	:	I see myself enjoying my studies and work.
Self Affirmation	:	I am enjoying learning.
Change Area	:	I want to be confident and focused.
Image	:	I see my self performing or dancing on the floor.
Self Affirmation	:	I am confident and focused.
Change Area	:	I want to be fit and fine.
Image	:	I see my self running.
Self Affirmation	:	I am fit and fine.

Change Area : I want to take control of my life.

Image : I see my self driving a BMW car

Self Affirmation : I have total control over my life.

Change Area : I want to become a Doctor, Engineer, Teacher, IAS............. or whatever you want.

Image : I see myself as a Doctor, Engineer, Teacher, IAS.......... Or whatever you want to become .

Self Affirmation : I am a Doctor, Engineer, Teacher, IAS .... or whatever you want to become.

(So, you identify the change areas and your self affirmations with corresponding image. You have to see your images while verbalising your self affirmations. Your affirmations must be in present tense. It can be 6-10 at one time)

Mind Power Reprogramming

Step – 1

Verbalise

6-10

Self-affirmations

Morning–Evening

Atleast

6 times in a gap of 6 sec.

(In every 21 days, you may re-identify the change areas and accordingly write corresponding self-affirmations with images and keep on verbalising)

Mind Power Reprogramming

Step – 2

Visualise

Self-affirmation

(Morning–Evening)

(Sit comfortably, close your eyes and take three deep breaths. Start visualising your self-affirmations and your dreams by creating corresponding your happy, winning and positive images.)

Because

If you can

See it

You can

Have it

Mind Power Reprogramming

Step – 3

Visualising your self-affirmation and dreams

As if it has already happened,

Will make it happen in reality

With

FEELINGS

Mind is a Goal Seeking Machine which doesn't understand the language of words but of images with feelings. You have to tell lie to your Mind, if you want to be happy and fine irrespective of your size, colour, family background, religion and present conditions. Suppose, you are not scoring good marks in mathematics or any subject and want to improve your performance, start seeing and visualising that you have already scored 90% marks in that subject with smile on your face. Though you are not scoring 90% marks presently. This is fact. Please remember, your Mind has nothing to do with facts. It only understands what you want with feeling. So, whatever you want, see yourself that you have already got that with a feeling of success and you will get in reality. This is a process and you too can become master of this art if you practice for minimum 90 days.

If you are not happy, tell your Mind all the time, while sitting, walking, eating and before sleeping that you are happy with smile on your face, you will become happy. This may take some time. You have to be patient. If you want to become a Doctor, start seeing and visualising yourself as a Doctor all the time and within a few months and years you will become a Doctor. The same way you can achieve whatever you want in your life.

Now, you don't ask me, how it works? I can't say. But, this is true. Start dreaming, thinking, feeling, seeing, doing as what you want to become and you will become in reality. That's why it is said, THOUGHTS ARE THINGS.

Have you not heard one mantra of purification from your Priest?

Om apavitrah pavitrova sarvawasthang gato api wa, yah smaret pundari kakchhang sa bahyadhyantrah shuchih, shuchih.

This means, whether you are pure or impure, good or bad, black or white, Hindu or Muslim, just take some water in your hand, close your eyes & think and assume that you are pure and clean and throw that water over your body and surroundings. Everything including you will become pure and clean. Again this proves that everything is in Mind — success and failure, fear and courage, happiness and disappointments and richness and poverty. The choice is yours.

What you think all the time, you will become that only.

In arithmetic too, when you solve a sum you have to assume the result first then you get the actual result. Isn't it? MIND works like this only. Around 87% people on this earth don't use their MIND throughout their life and blame everything for their conditions. This is the BIGGEST surprise on this EARTH.

Start each day with
Visualising and seeing what you want,
See yourself handling every responsibility
Effectively as a student.
Believe in yourself that what you want
Has already happened, though in reality
It is yet to happen.
See yourself moving through the day with a smile
On your face and joy in your heart.

Eventually, what you have seen happening, will happen!

– Anonymous

Verbalise

Visualise

Emotionalise

Your

Dreams

And

Pray, pray, pray, pray..................

(This will connect your MIND with the UNIVERSAL MIND and All +ve forces, thoughts, things, people and circumstances related to your Dream will rush towards you to help you to make you SUCCESSFUL & HAPPY!)

Because

You are **waiting** that God is going to help you,

And

God is waiting that you will **declare** your dreams by recreating picture images in your subconscious mind,

So that HE could help you to make you

SUCCESSFUL!

You can't just sit there and wait for success to fall in your lap; once your dream is set and your will is firm, you have to make a practical effort. Then you will see that whatever you require for success starts coming to you. Everything will push you in the right direction your divinely surcharged willpower is the answer to your prayer. When you use that will, you open the way through which your prayers can be answered.

– Sri Sri Paramahansa Yogananda

LIFE

is a mystery

To be **explored**

Not a problem

To be **solved.**

– Anonymous

This "MANKIND" can be divided in two classes. One, who take birth and pass the time to meet their DEATH. They don't have any idea about their LIFE. This type of "MAN" lives his life assuming life as a PROBLEM. They spend their life in solving it. They use to visit Mandir, Masjid, Gurudwara, Church, Astrologers, Pundits, Doctors, Psychologists, Numerologists to find solutions. They never think or take their life differently. They don't enquire within to find the ANSWER.

The second one, who take birth assuming their life as "SEED". They nourish and explore their whole life; this "SEED" into "PLANT", full of flowers and fruits. They never wait for their death but, enjoy their life journey. They love their life. They don't have time to think about death. They keep themselves busy in EXPLORING their LIFE.

You don't need to know "How" you are actually going to achieve your **dreams**, when you make it. Just repeatedly visualise the end results and

The "HOW" will open to you.

– Vince Pfaff

Once a journalist asked Sachin Tendulkar, "How could you play cricket for such a long period successfully?" Sachin replied with smile on his face, "I don't know. I just play one day at a time and give my 100%, that's all I have been doing. Rest of the things have been taken care by GOD. I am myself surprised how I played so long. One thing I know that I always love myself, my cricket and my dreams."

I also realised the same thing, when I lost everything in business. Everything was looking gloomy and dark. I was kicked out from my in-law's house. All so called friends became enemies. I spoke to myself what to do, now? I talked to my SAI for guidance. I came to New Delhi. I joined one cosmetic company as Chief Executive Officer (CEO). But, I could not continue there as I was not enjoying and resigned. Again, it looked that all roads were closed for me. Again I asked myself what to do now and I got the answer. I gave serious and different thinking. I evaluated my SWORD and I got again one road that is TRAINING and MOTIVATING youths, parents and teachers.

I remember that day was 6th June'09, when I conducted my first seminar on "I LUV MYSELF" at Kerala Public school, New Delhi. Only six students attended that seminar. When I came to know that I have to give lecture to six students only, I got a bit demotivated. But, I put my 100% in that seminar. I can't forget those 6 students, 6th June, 6th sens and Kerala Public School, new Delhi in my whole life. Since then I have conducted more than 150 seminars / workshops across India and abroad & trained and motivated more than 60,000 students / teacher and parents. I don't know how this happened! But I can tell you with great authority that you don't need to know "HOW" you are actually going to achieve your dream. If at all you have to ask, ask what should I do to achieve my dream! You just focus on what you want to achieve. That's all. "HOW" will keep on emerging in front of you in course of your journey.

What is proven today

Was once **imagined** only!

– Anonymous

Think, Feel & Imagine,

while going through your life!

A man was walking down a country road and came across a field in which three people were breaking up large boulders with hammers. He asked the first man, what he is doing. The man replied, "Can't you see? I am breaking stones!" He turned up to the second man and asked the same question. The second man replied, "Can't you see? I am doing my job!" Now came the turn of the third one. He replied, "Can't you see? I am building a beautiful temple!"

What are you doing? write a few sentences about your thinking, feeling & doing about yourself!

....

....

....

....

....

Name : Signature :

What you are receiving today is the result of the choices you have made in the past.

If you keep on **doing** what you have always done,

you will keep on **getting** what you have always got.

– Jack Canfield

All men and women are born, live, suffer and die;

What distinguishes us from another is our dreams,
whether they are dreams about worldly or unworldly
things and what we do to make them come about.
We don't choose to be born. We don't choose our parents.
We don't choose our country of birth, our colour, religion.
We don't choose to die.
We don't choose the time and conditions of our death.

But

We do choose how we live.

– Joseph Epstein

You have to give up

Blaming!

Most of the youths are suffering from this cancerous disease, which is known as "BLAMITUS & EXCUSITUS". As per my own life experience and research on over 40,000 youths across India and abroad, I can say with authority and sincerity that these cancerous diseases are due to overgrowth of one harmful bacteria, i.e. "I LUV YOU".

All blames are waste of time.
No matter how much
fault you find with others and regardless of
how much you blame them,

it will not change

YOU.

– Wayne Dyer

You

will never get SUCCESS

as long as you continue to

BLAME

other people and circumstances

for your failure!

You are the one who never listened to your parents!

You are the one who bunked the classes and tuitions!

You are the one who abused the teachers and friends!

You are the one who wasted time on TV, Internet and Mobile!

You are the one who gossiped and partied!

You are the one who scored poor marks!

You are the one who lost trust of your parents and teachers!

You are the one who failed!

You are the one who started taking alcohol and drugs!

You are the one who landed in

hospital or jail!

This is because of choices you made.

So, who is to blame?

What you should do?

You

just take

total **responsibility**

of your activities from **today** and **right now!**

Take a deep breath and start praying for change in yourself.

No great life was ever built on a foundation of

BLAMES & EXCUSES.

So, stop making them!

You will surprise to know that this ordinary man, who used to sell plastic cups in a small town of America, achieved extraordinary success when reached the age of 60. He was very ordinary and insecure till 58. He never thought differently and abstractly about himself. One fine afternoon when he was standing in a 'Q' to eat 'BURGER' in front of a restaurant, this ordinary looking man started enquiring about him and thinking differently. He rediscovered himself. What he could not think in 58 years, he thought in one hour. He did his SWORD analysis. He started taking steps with confidence. He never reached RIGHT place at RIGHT time till 58. But the moment he recreated his winning picture images of his dreams and started loving himself, he started reaching RIGHT places at RIGHT time, started enjoying and started getting SUCCESS. Today, who doesn't know MC DONALD'S & it's delicious BURGERS. This ordinary, insecure man was Ray Kroc, who brought a revolution in restaurant chain business world wide and given a success formulae.

So, as a **responsible** student and person,

You must obey the Mcdonald's chairman Ray Kroc's

Principles of Success.

- Reach right place at the right time.
- Stay there for sometime.
- Do something there.

So

- **Reach your schools/tutions at the right time.**
- **Stay there with your mind and body for 5-6 hrs.**
- **Give your 100% there.**

Don't think what other people, your friends, your loved ones, think of you. All that matters is what you think of you. Don't waste time in taking your friend's approval but take self approval.

Love yourself,

Respect yourself

and your decisions.

Don't try to become POPULAR but,

Try to focus your entire energy to make yourself

BIG in front of your EYES only .

The entire world will start loving, respecting and praising you.

Don't wait for ideal CIRCUMSTANCES;

They never come.

– Janet stuart

I have heard one eye opening story in my school days. Four friends set out for a pilgrimage with one Fakir. They begged whole day and collected some rupee. All four friends requested the Fakir to fetch some sweets from nearby market. The Fakir went to market and brought some Halwa. But halwa's quantity was less and was not enough to make their belly full. So, they started arguing. The argument turned into a big fight. They were not in a position to decide who would take how much halwa. So, they requested the Fakir to decide. The Fakir suggested to go for sleep without eating halwa as the night was approaching and in the morning they would brief about their dreams. Whoever would see the best dream, would take the bigger share in halwa. All five slept and woke up in the morning with their dreams. The first man said that he had seen in his dream that God was standing in front of him and saying that he was my lovely child and no one was like him on this earth. So, he claimed that he deserved the halwa. The second friend said about his dream. Third, fourth and the Fakir's turn came at last. Fakir said that God had come in his dream and said, "Son awake! Eat halwa." So, I ate all halwa. How could I disobey God's order.

So friends, don't laugh but start eating your part of halwa, i.e your life. And this is possible only when you love yourself. Stop evaluating others. Start focusing on yourself. Don't wait for tomorrow, it never comes. Give your 100% toady. This will improve your self image and you will feel good about yourself.

So, **CHANGE** your self-image!

By

Chanting all the time

I LUV MYSELF

Within.

(This is the mantra for success)

Stop saying "I Love You" to your opposite sex during 12-18 years, as the process of making you a man or a woman is going on in your system.

This period is called "SWADHYAY".

SWA : Self

ADHYAY : Awareness

"I luv you", this statement is full of lust and greed. This statement is not real and has any truth or meaning. If father loves his son, brother loves his brother and sister, mother loves her child, wife loves her husband, husband loves his wife and this world is full of love then from where this violence, hatred, anger do come? Why every where every one is fighting! Since last 3000 years, 14000 battles are fought!

I also used this statement "I LUV YOU" very often. I always said this statement to my mother when I was in school but never loved her during my school days. I never obeyed her. I never cared her but fooled her all the time and played with her emotions by using this false statement "I LUV YOU, MOM". Today, when I lost my, mom, I realised the meaning of this statement.

When I reached college, I kept on loving others: my boy friends, girl friends. I used to sit hours and hours with my so called friends whom I loved. I always compromised with my priorities. I never focused on my studies as I was busy in gossiping, roaming and chatting. And this resulted in poor performance in college. When I started my business enterprises, I did the same thing again. In every business meetings I used this statement "I LUV YOU colleagues". But, in return everybody took this statement as my weakness. I always cared for my fellow employees and associates but, nobody loved me. This resulted in poor productivity and losses. I loved my business partners and they fooled and cheated me. I lost my business, my parental and self earned properties and my self-esteem.

I loved my relatives and I was kicked on my ass. I trusted and loved everybody and I was deceived by everyone, I loved.

After losing everything, I realised that "I luv you" is the mantra of failure, frustration, disappointment and poverty. So, never say "I luv you" to anybody unless, "you know yourself and love yourself".

You love yourself, respect yourself, and trust yourself first before declaring your love to others, then only your Godly power, creative power will guide you to success.

When you die and go to heaven, God will ask you,

"why don't you become

YOU?"

– Anonymous

I have to remember to tell the negative committee

that meets in my head all the time to

Sit down

and

SHUT UP.

– Kathy Kendall

There are many things in LIFE that will catch your eyes,

but only a few will catch your heart.

Pursue them.

– Anonymous

Before creating your **Dreams,**

Answer the following questions:

What is important to you?

What do you feel passionate about?

What interests you most?

What values are most important to you?

What do you want to accomplish?

What do you want to contribute?

What do you believe in?

What is your potential?

What are your strengths?

How do you like to be remembered?

If you believe in yourself,

your God and your dreams;

You can make it

possible.

It doesn't necessarily make it easy.

Ask Now

Do you **love** yourself?

Are you ready to **LIVE** your dreams?

To accomplish
your dreams,
You have to start

writing,

believing,

striving,

dreaming,

changing,

becoming

feeling

and

living

your

DREAMS!

Doctor

Leader

Cricketer

Mentor

Manager

Teacher

Dancer

Engineer

What are your dreams?

Advocate

Film maker

Politician

Singer

IAS officer

CA/CS

Nurse

Social worker

Actor

Businessman

Life's Dream Plan

1. PERSONAL :

- I am living a fulfilling life beyond the age of 90.
- I am joining Gym/Dance classes/Aerobic classes.
- I am listening to instrumental music for atleast 10 minutes daily in the evening.
-
-
-

2. PROFESSIONAL :

- I am scoring more than 80% marks in my 10th board exams by March 2011.
- I am scoring more than 85% marks in my 11th final exams by March 2012.
- I am scoring more than 85% marks in my 12th board exams by March 2013.
- I am getting admission in professional college of my choice by July 2013.
- I am a professional (Doctor, Engineer, Teacher ....) by July 2018.
-
-
-

3. FAMILY :

- I am getting married at the age of 28-30 (for boys) and 24-26 (for girls).
- I am having one beautiful girl/boy child by the age of 35.
- I am financially independent by the age of 40.
- I am building a sprawling house by the age of 45.
-
-
-
-
-

4. SPIRITUAL :

- I am giving 15 minutes everyday in instalments to my God.
- I am tithing atleast 10% of my pocket money weekly/monthly.
- I am giving my one hour time daily/weekly in educating poor and downtrodden.
- I am visiting atleast one pilgrimage station with my family and parents every year from the age of 35.
-
-
-

(This is a model life's dream plan. You can write your own life's dream plan. This dream is to be prepared in present tense only, as if the dreams are already achieved. Fix this dream list in your bedroom and verbalise, visualise and emotionalise all your dreams, as soon as you wake up in the morning and when you retire to your bed at night. It will take hardly 15 minutes daily. You will be surprised after 365 days!)

Who is your

Role Model?

(Select one Role Model except your parents. Your parents are your biological Role Models and they are always with you.)

Role Models

are very important as they have already achieved

what you want to achieve in your life.

So, you just have to select one role model for yourself

like whom you want to be and

start imitating him/her.

When I was in school in 1980's, I wanted to be a musician and singer. I couldn't select a Role Model at that time. Moreover, there was lack of awareness too. No one was available there who could guide me in selecting a Role Model for me. Still, I feel a great singer, musician is crying within me.

When I came to Varanasi in Udai Pratap Inter College, this singer within me started growing. I always participated in all stage programmes in college. Twice, I won All inter state singing competition. But, I couldn't select a Role Model here too. And, the singer within me died prematurely. Many a time, I skipped my classes in college for this singing passion, which resulted poor performance in studies. I missed 1st class in my plus-two exam by one marks.

When I started my professional career as Sales Representative in a pharmaceutical company, i.e. SYSTOPIC, I realised the importance of a professional Role Model. Here I didn't waste my time in selecting it. My first Role Model is Mr. Sunny Arora , who was my first Boss in SYSTOPIC and presently working as Vice President at INTAS Pharmaceuticals Ltd. Ahmedabad. I learned ABC of sales and marketing from him. He made me a smart salesman. I learned professional etiquettes and manners from him. He is my first professional GURU.

THEN, I met my first Managing Director, Mr. PK Dutta and astonished by his assertive, affable style. I started acting like him. I started imitating his style in my day to day professional life. I learned assertiveness, sales closing techniques, leadership skills from him without attending any MBA School. I salute both of them.

I was inspired by Mr. PK Dutta immensely. I started my own pharma co. later in my professional life because of his inspiration. Though I couldn't become a successful Managing Director like my Role Model, Mr. PK Dutta. However, whatever I am today, it is because of him only.

I couldn't forget one incidence of my professional career. I was working as Area Manager in Biological E. Ltd at Patna. I was busy in my sales closing on that day. I saw Mr. PK Dutta, my Role Model there. The office of SYSTOPIC was in the same building of Biologicals at Patna those days. I was surprised. I had not expected him there. My Role model was standing in front of me. You couldn't fathom my happiness. I touched his feet. He hugged me. Whenever I feel disheartened in my life, I just bring that image in front of my eyes and get encouragement from my Role Model.

You must have seen “IQBAL”, a Hindi film. This entire film is based on visualization, self affirmation, role modeling, dream and success. There was a deaf village boy who wanted to become a fast bowler like kapildev, the great Indian cricketer. Iqbal was a poor boy. His father wanted to make him a farmer. He always compeled him to accompany in all farming activities. But Iqbal always wanted to be like his Role Model, Kapil Dev. He used to talk to his Role Model’s photograph. He always visualised that he had achieved his dream of playing for India as fast bowler at Eden Garden, Kolkata and his Role Model, Kapil Dev had come to meet him. Day in day out he had been visualising for years and ultimately, Kapil Dev came to meet him at Eden Gardens in the last scene in the film. This happens all the time not in films only. You just have enough “shraddha” and “saburi” in self and your GOD. If you have not seen this film, you should watch. This will change your perception.

Keep on **imitating**

Your role model!

(All successful people have imitated their role models initially and in the process they themselves became role models.)

Barack Obama,

today's American President

IMITATING

Abraham Lincoln,

the great American President.

Moreover, he is inspired by Mahatma Gandhi and Martin Luther King Jr. too.

Positive Role Model

There was a man in this world, who always believed in himself and who has become a role model for millions of strugglers, poor and stressful people across the world. He is none other than Abraham Lincoln. His resume is:

Age 22 : Failed in business.

Age 23 : Ran for legislature and defeated.

Age 24 : Failed again in business.

Age 25 : Ran for legislature and elected.

Age 26 : His girlfriend died.

Age 27 : Met a nervous breakdown.

Age 29 : Ran for speaker and defeated.

Age 31 : Ran for elector and defeated.

Age 34 : Ran for Congress and defeated.

Age 37 : Elected to Congress.

Age 39 : Ran for Congress and defeated.

Age 46 : Defeated for senate.

Age 47 : Defeated for Vice President.

Age 49 : Defeated for Senate.

Age 51 : Elected President of the United States of America.

Abraham Lincoln never bothered what people used to say about him, when he **failed.**

He always **failed forward.** Whenever he failed, he asserted himself that he was born to accomplish something else

and immediately started thinking for the next position.

Even when he became the **President**, people still criticised him but instead of becoming stressful; he expressed his powerful statement,

"No one is good enough to be President but someone has to be. So, why not me!"

Decide

what you want to be,

Select

like whom you want to be,

Start

IMITATING

and

You will become

what you want to be!

(Fix a big size photograph of your role model in your bedroom and visualise that you have already become like him and he has come to congratulate you.)

While making your dreams

and selecting your

ROLE MODEL

Follow ....

THINKING

About what you want to be?

FEELING

How would you feel when you realise your dreams?

DOING

What are the steps you are taking to realise your dreams?

But the moment you decide and

PLUNGE

for accomplishing your dreams ....

Change the order.

DOING

Start taking actions step by step to realise your dreams!
Make a POSITIVE momentum.

THINKING

While doing, you will encounter with problems. Keep on thinking on better options to solve them and keep on asking for help and move on! Always think that the entire UNIVERSE is working for you to make you SUCCESSFUL. You are a POWER. Nobody can defeat you except your own defeating thoughts and images.

FEELING

While doing, thinking and solving the problems, feel the taste of success to get motivated! Always feel that you have already achieved your Dream.

SUCCEEDING

Now, you are a winner. You have achieved your Dream. It might have taken months and years. But you are successful. Now, you are a SUPER STAR.

You are a born

SUPERSTAR

You need to learn skills and acquire

STYLE and STARDOM

(Think, Feel and Do)

365 DAYS STARDOM PROGRAMME

(Factors of stardom)

Check your score today and start improving everyday and become a star in just 365 days.

BALANCE

Winners have full lives, paying attention to personal, family, professional and spiritual development.

0 1 2 3 4 5 6 7 8 9 10

What is your score today :

Score Tracking

30 days	60 days	120 days	180 days	270 days	365 days

BALANCE

Is the key to **SUCCESS** in all things. Don't neglect your

Mind, Body and Spirit.

Invest **TIME** and **energy** in all of them equally – it will be the best investment you ever make,

not just for **YOUR LIFE** but for whatever is to follow.

– Tanya Wheway

DO SOME ACTIVITY HERE TO BRING CHANGES IN YOUR THOUGHT PATTERN:

Are you BALANCED and paying attention to your MIND, BODY and SPIRIT? Write your self analysis:

- **What are you doing daily to nurish your MIND:**....................

....

....

....

....

- **What are you doing daily to keep your BODY fit:**.................

....

....

....

- **What are you doing daily to renew your SPIRIT:**

....

....

....

....

DREAM

Winners have strong sense of purpose and they work their life from a specific plan.

0 1 2 3 4 5 6 7 8 9 10

What is your score today :

Score Tracking

30 days	60 days	120 days	180 days	270 days	365 days

An effective **goal** focusses primarily on **results** rather than **activity**. It identifies where you want to be, and in the process helps you determine where you are. It gives you important information on **how** to get there and it tells you when you have arrived. It unifies your efforts or energy. It gives meaning and purpose to all you do.

– Stephen R. Covey

All who have accomplished great things have had a great aim, have fixed their gaze on a goal which was high, one which sometimes seemed impossible...

— Orison Swett Marden

DO SOME ACTIVITY HERE TO BRING CHANGES IN YOUR THOUGHT PATTERN:

What are your dreams and purposes in life? Write something about your life plans:

- **Immediate dream plan:**

1

2

3

4

- **Intermediate dream plan:**

1

2

3

4

- **Life's cherished dream plan:**

1

2

3

4

Dream Card

Suppose your dream is to become an IIT engineer from IIT, Kharagpur. This dream card will be of great help.

Er. Ravi Software Engg.	Mob. 9576553860
affix your colour photo	
Indian Institute of Technology, Kharagpur, India	

Today, you are in std 11th. You are not an engineer. You want to become an engineer from IIT Kharagpur. This dream card will help you in achieving your dream. You have to watch this card at least 20 times in a day for 90 days with feelings that you have already become an engineer from IIT kharagpur. Keep this card near your heart. This gives you graphics to continually saturate your mind with the rewards you will enjoy as you progress towards your dreams. This will help you to focus on your priority areas.

It is rightly said, "out of sight – out of mind." Your dreams are easier to achieve if you keep them insight. For keeping your dream always in your sight, make your dream card in advance as if you have already achieved your dream. After practising this psychological exercise for 90 days, keep this dream card in locker or in some safe place. After one year or two, you again open your locker and bring out this card. You would be surprised to see the results. You don't ask me "how" but it works.

DELAYED GRATIFICATION

Winners fully understand the law of harvesting. Seeds planted today must be carefully nurtured to bear fruits tomorrow. They are able to work hard on a fixed goal. They never become impulsive for instant gratification.

0 1 2 3 4 5 6 7 8 9 10

What is your score today :

Score Tracking

30 days	60 days	120 days	180 days	270 days	365 days

There are no **shortcuts** in life.

Instant gratification takes too long.

– Carrie Fisher

You would not start earning 50,000 dollars a year as soon as you come out of high school. You would become a CEO with car, mobile and laptop, until you earn and it will take time and your dedicated and goal-focussed effort.

– MANUKUL

Do some activities

How many times did you make shortcuts to get something? What are your experiences about instant gratification? write something about your shortcut stories, experiences and outcomings:

....
....
....
....
....
....
....
....
....

POSITIVE THINKER

Winners are positive thinkers. Because of their goal-oriented approach, they can't afford to be negative but at the same time they are realistic.

0 1 2 3 4 5 6 7 8 9 10

What is your score today :

Score Tracking

30 days	60 days	120 days	180 days	270 days	365 days

POSITIVE OR NEGATIVE

Thinking

It

Is an individual's

CHOICE!

When you are **thinking positive**, you are generating

1/10 volt of **electricity**

which makes your **mind** work efficiently.

As soon as you start thinking negative, the electricity

generation increases and

if not controlled by ALTERING your thoughts, may damage

your heart, kidney, mind or even your entire life.

Choice is yours!

– MANUKUL

Do some activities

Do you think negative or positive? Write all your negative thoughts and alter them with positive self affirmation :

- Negative thoughts : ....

  Image : ....

  Positive Self Affirmation : ....

- Negative thoughts : ....

  Image : ....

Positive Self Affirmation : ....

- Negative thoughts : ....

  Image : ....

Positive Self Affirmation : ....

- Negative thoughts : ....

  Image : ....

Positive Self Affirmation : ....

CONFIDENT

Winners have the confidence to forge ahead without needing the approval of their peers. Winners have complete belief in their abilities, often without any proof to achieve their goal.

0 1 2 3 4 5 6 7 8 9 10

What is your score today :

Score Tracking

30 days	60 days	120 days	180 days	270 days	365 days

What you SEE and **expect**

from yourself with **confidence,**

you usually get it.

Do some activities

Write down the obstacles and difficulties in your path to achieve your dream :

1 ....

2 ....

3 ....

4 ....

5 ....

6 ....

Now, affirm that you are overcoming all the above obstacles and difficultiesby chanting within, “I am confident and focused.”

CHARACTER

Winners are the men of character. Character means the kind of person you truly are – not what others say about you and this radiates from your face and body language. Even in failure and severe criticism, winners never lose their focus.

0 1 2 3 4 5 6 7 8 9 10

What is your score today :

Score Tracking

30 days	60 days	120 days	180 days	270 days	365 days

A person's **true** character is revealed by what he does when NO ONE else is watching.

– Anonymous

The **ultimate** measure of a man is not where he stands in moments of *comfort*, but where he stands at times of challenge and controversies.

– Martin Luther King Jr.

DO SOME ACTIVITIES

Write your story when you faced challenges and controversies. Also, write your experiences when you came out of that situation:

....
....
....
....
....
....
....
....

"I LUV MYSELF" FACTOR

Your "I Luv Myself" factor means how much you love yourself. This continues to grow as you keep on winning. This is earned and inculcated.

0 1 2 3 4 5 6 7 8 9 10

What is your score today:

Score Tracking

30 days	60 days	120 days	180 days	270 days	365 days

When you tell YOURSELF good or told you are good, you should not relax but should try to become even BETTER.

Your continuous *improvement* gives happiness to you, to those around you and to God.

– Sri Sri Paramahansa Yogananda

This world would not care about your self-esteem. You have to love and respect yourself on your own, if you really want to be a

winner and successful.

– MANUKUL

DO SOME ACTIVITIES

Write one incident of your life when you loved yourself very much and you felt WOW on yourself. Also write something about the outcome of that incident:

....

....

....

....

....

....

POSITIVE SELF-IMAGE

Winners have the ability to see themselves winning well in advance. Their self-image is in harmony with their goals.

0 1 2 3 4 5 6 7 8 9 10

What is your score today:

Score Tracking

30 days	60 days	120 days	180 days	270 days	365 days

The **self-image** is the key to human personality and behaviour. But more than this, self-image sets the **boundaries** of individuals' accomplishments. It defines what

you can and can't be.

– Maltz

"only 7% of what you communicate to others is in the form of words. 38% comes from your tone of voice while the other 55% is represented by your body language including your facial expression, general posture and various body movements."

Do some activities

Fill in the blanks :

- Yes, I can solve my problems.
- Yes, I can score 95% marks in physics.
- Yes, I can ....
- Yes, I can ....
- Yes, I can ....
- Yes, I can ....
- Yes, I can ....
- Yes, I can ....
- Yes, I can ....
- Yes, I can ....
- Yes, I can ....

SELF-DISCIPLINE

Discipline means taking control of your activities. This possesses the magic of self-motivation. When discipline is linked to goal, success naturally follows. Good study habits, good work habits, exercise habits, food habits and good time management are elements of self-discipline.

0 1 2 3 4 5 6 7 8 9 10

What is your score today:

Score Tracking

30 days	60 days	120 days	180 days	270 days	365 days

DISCIPLINE makes a person great.

– Indira Gandhi

When you are hard and tough on yourself, life will be easy on you but when you are easy on yourself, life will be HARD on you.

– Zig Ziglar

Do some activities

Write your good habits:

1

2

3

4

5

6

Write your bad habits :

1

2

3

4

5

6

COURAGE

Nothing ventured, nothing achieved. Winners always take risks and are willing to fail forward in order to succeed.

0 1 2 3 4 5 6 7 8 9 10

What is your score today:

Score Tracking

30 days	60 days	120 days	180 days	270 days	365 days

LIFE IS NOTHING BUT A RISK!

To laugh is to risk appearing a fool.

To weep is to risk appearing sentimental.

To reach for another is to risk involvement.

To expose your feelings is to risk exposing your true self.

To place your ideas and dreams before a crowd is to risk their loss.

To love is to risk not being loved in return.

To live is to risk dying.

To believe is to risk despair.

To try is to risk failure.

But **risks** must be taken, because the greatest hazard
in life is to risk nothing. You may avoid suffering
and sorrow but you can't learn,
feel, change, grow, love and live.
Chained by your attitude you are slaves;
You have **forfeited** your freedom.
Only a person who take risks is

FREE.

– Anonymous Teacher

Do some activities

Write at least one risk you had taken this year and got success:

....
....
....
....
....

HEALTH and FITNESS

People who get most out of their life need high level of energy. They can't afford to get sick and invite needless fatigue. Thus, they always keep themselves fit and fine.

0 1 2 3 4 5 6 7 8 9 10

What is your score today:

Score Tracking

30 days	60 days	120 days	180 days	270 days	365 days

Your body will **honour** you with wellness,

if you honour it with **awareness.**

– Anonymous

DO SOME ACTIVITIES

Are you fit and fine? What are the secrets of your fitness? If you are not fit and fine and feel lethargy all the time, what are you doing to be fit & fine:

....
....
....
....
....
....
....
....

AVOID NEGATIVE COMPANY

Winners learn the art how to avoid the company of negative people. Winners associate with winners only.

0 1 2 3 4 5 6 7 8 9 10

What is your score today:

Score Tracking

30 days	60 days	120 days	180 days	270 days	365 days

MISERY LOVES COMPANY.

This is a negative world. The more you go for searching friends outside, the more you would get false friends and true enemies. Between the age of 12-18 years, make your parents your best friends. You will never get true friends like them. Love them without expecting love in return.

– MANUKUL

DO SOME ACTIVITIES

Are you associated with good and positive people around you? Name them and why do you think they are positive and good?

....
....
....
....
....
....

PERSISTENT

Winners always finish what they start. They don't blame others. They keep on working sometimes against great odds. They don't make excuses.

0 1 2 3 4 5 6 7 8 9 10

What is your score today:

Score Tracking

30 days	60 days	120 days	180 days	270 days	365 days

Fix a Goal,

Never Give Up until

you achieve.

DO SOME ACTIVITIES

Write one incident of your life when did you achieve your goal against great odds:

....

....

....

....

....

EMPOWERMENT

All winners know that power can be taken, not given. The process of mastering 'knowing yourself' is empowerment.

0 1 2 3 4 5 6 7 8 9 10

What is your score today :

Score Tracking

30 days	60 days	120 days	180 days	270 days	365 days

Knowing others is intelligence.

Knowing yourself is true wisdom.

Mastering others is strength.

Mastering yourself is
true power.

– Tao te Ching

DO SOME ACTIVITIES

Do you know yourself? write something about yourself:

....

....

....

....

....

....

HUMAN RULE

Winners treat people the way they would like to be treated. Their success is not at the cost of other people. What you send out – comes back to you. What you sow – you reap. What you give – you get. What you see in others – exists in you.

0 1 2 3 4 5 6 7 8 9 10

What is your score today:

Score Tracking

30 days	60 days	120 days	180 days	270 days	365 days

Live,

Let **others** Live too.

What you don't want done to yourself, don't do to others.

– Confucius

DO SOME ACTIVITIES

Do you always treat others the way you would like to be treated? Write one incident when you were not treated well and humiliated:

……………………………………………………………………………………………

……………………………………………………………………………………………

……………………………………………………………………………………………

……………………………………………………………………………………………

……………………………………………………………………………………………

WINNER
VS
LOSER

The **Winner** – is always part of the answer.

The Loser – is always part of the problem.

The Winner – always has a programme.

The Loser – always has an excuse.

The Winner – says "let me do it for you".

The Loser – says "that's not my job".

The Winner – sees an answer to every problem.

The Loser – sees a problem in every answer.

The Winner – sees a green near every sand trap.

The Loser – sees two or three sand traps near every green.

The Winner – says "it may be difficult but it's possible".

The Loser – says "it may be easy but it's too difficult".

BE A WINNER!

Category of Students

INSECURE FELLOW

They are always insecure and afraid that they might fail.

As they always think about failure, they never get started. They always think, feel and do negative things. They always seek false security and help. Basically, they don't love themselves. Majority of them live their life in mediocrity. One among them who loved himself was Mr. Ray Kroc, Mcdonald's chairman. He was very insecure till 58 and became successful at the age of 60.

Adolf Hitler, Saddam Hussain, Bin Laden, Dawood Ibrahim are the most insecure fellows because they don't love themselves. All criminals, terrorists, kidnappers are the most insecure pople. They never love themselves. Ratnakar, Angulimal are the rare names who converted themselves when they started loving themselves in later part of their life and became ROLE MODELS for entire humanity.

If you are the dignified member of this club then become impatient and use W7H. This impatience will bring change in your THINKING, FEELING & DOING! Start loving yourself. If not, life will become a burden and problem for you and others.

For this club members, who don't love themselves, the UNIVERSAL INFINITE POWER and SPEED work against them. If they fail to bring changes in their THINKING, majority are killed prematurely.

LAZY FELLOW

They are always busy in enjoying the fun and pleasures o. life. They always plan to do something but tomorrow. They always think that life is made for fun and pleasure not for work. They keep themselves busy roaming, gossiping and partying with their false friends. They always believe that life will continue like the way they are leading at this moment. They waste their time and money of their parents. They are showy fellows. They keep themselves busy in loving and pleasing others. Basically, they don't love themselves.

They start loving themselves when they reach 40. By this age they usually have visited hospital or jail many a time. This lot always inclined to accumulate wealth through any means. They start getting SUCCESS after 40, when they start loving themselves.

This club members spend their valuable time watching TV, chatting on internet and mobile. This club members live in their false psudo world that they have created only from TV and INTERNET.

If you are a dignified member of this club, stop watching TV and INTERNET. Don't use MOBILE until you turn 18. TV, Internet and Mobile are lazy making machines.

BLAMING FELLOW

They are who always say that I have tried many times but I could not succeed. I have tried to quit smoking but could not because of my friends. They are argumentative people. They always try to prove their point of view right. If they fail they blame somebody else even school, teacher, circumstances for their failure.They always blame people, conditions and circumstances. They know what they are doing but they have decided not to do anything to change themselves. Basically, they don't love themselves.

They start loving themselves when they reach 35, after losing many things in life. This lot is a vulnerable lot. They often think and feel that they are the smartest fellows. They believe in fooling others. They live in their false perception. But when they reach 35, they start loving themselves and after wards they grow very fast in their life. They reach to the TOP in their selected area/ field.

Majority of this lot are politicians, advocates, consultants and entrepreneurs. This club members are advised to stop gossiping, chatting and roaming. They are also advised to talk less so that they could get the opportunity to listen to their own inner voice, i.e. GOD's voice.

FOOLISH FELLOW

They are who have some idea, plan for their life but they always procrastinate. They cannot take decisions for themselves at right time as they are always concerned what others, their friends would think and say! They are procrastinating fellows. They have ignition problem. They live their life in tomorrow. Basically, they don't love themselves. They are quick learners but poor listners.

They start loving themselves when they reach 20-25 after getting some humiliation, set backs and failures. They get SUPER SUCCESS afterwards. They earn name, fame, health, wealth, prosperity not only for themselves but for others too after 30.

This club members should not waste time in worrying. They should learn from their mistakes. They should learn the skills and art to avoid procrastination at the earliest. If they are not overcoming this habit, you will step into LAZY or BLAMMERS club.

WISE & INTELLIGENT FELLOW

They are active people. They are “Do it now” people. No grass grows under their feet. They are born winners. They never waste time and idea. They always search for opportunities. They are proactive, disciplined and confident. They are performers. They know from beginning that they have potential to be winners. Because, they love themselves. They are born superstars. Sachin Tendulkar, Lata Mangeshkar, Bill Gates, Kapil Dev, AR Rahman, Abhinav Bindra, Shreya Ghoshal and many are from this wise & intelligent club.

My observations about today's students

FACTS

87% students THINK only but neither FEEL nor DO anything!

10% students THINK & FEEL only but never DO anything!

only 3% students THINK, FEEL, DO & SUCCEED!

FINDINGS

87% students are influenced and controlled by their EYES,

10% are influenced and controlled by their SKIN,NOSE AND TONGUE and

only 3% are influenced and controlled by their EARS.

- Those who are influenced and controlled by their EYES are always busy in thinking what others think about them. They are “I LUV YOU” people. They always suffer from Insecurity, Laziness, Excusitus and Blamitus. They never see within as they are busy in outer world. They are basically ordinary people. They lack leadership qualities. They are followers. They always live in their own false perception. They are afraid to face the reality.
- Those who are influenced and controlled by their NOSE, TONGUE and SKIN, are REACTIVE people. They are very sensitive. They always think that the entire world is working against them. They waste their valuable time in REACTING OR CRITICISING. They never respond or act. They are basically problem creators.
- Those who are influenced and controlled by their EARS, are winners and leaders. They always work on feedbacks

So, again I would like to sing a song for you" "Naino ki mat suniyo re, Naino ki mat maniyo, Naina thag lenge." Moreover, I feel you have not seriously or differently seen the following words:

LearN	**earN**	**Year**
Near	**Dear**	**Hear**
Fear	**Tear**	**EarTH**

All above words are made up with EAR. So use this equipment whenever you have to take a decision for yourself: close your EYES and put the question to your EARS and listen to your EARS. You will hear the soft voice of your GOD, who is within you. You focus your attention on your THROAT and HEART, while you are talking to your EARS. If your HEART is beating with normal speed and SALIVA is releasing in your THROAT, take the decision. But, while talking to your EARS if you feel dryness in THROAT and your HEART is beating fast, stop there. Don't take any decision.

This entire decision making process will take hardly one minute. The more you love yourself, the more decisive you will become. This is a process. Use your senses intelligently and take decisions by listening to the voice of your 6th SENSE through your EARS and be successful in life.

Ten Natural Laws for Students

Law of Abundance.

Law of Association.

Law of Communication.

Law of Tithing.

Law of Lemonade.

Law of *Karani* and *Bharani*.

Law of Belief

Law of Concentration

Law of Responsibility

Law of Attraction

LAW OF ABUNDANCE

"The essence of this law is that you must think abundance; see abundance; feel abundance, believe abundance. Let no thought of limitation enter your mind." — **Robert Gollier.**

God has given enough for everyone on this earth to achieve his/ her life's positive dream plans and enjoy his or her life. There is no scarcity. If there is any scarcity, that is in your mind.

I have observed that 85-90% students don't believe that they are born to accomplish something in their life. This is because of poor parenting. As per one data, children usually hear 1.5 lac times "NO" by the age of 14-15 years and only 100-150 times "YES" from their parents. Self image and "I LUV MYSELF" factor evaluated on the scale of 1-10 among 100 students (All were between 8-12 years), found very high. The average score was 8. The other set of students aged between 13-18 years were asked the same set of questions to evaluate their self image and "I LUV MYSELF" factors and they scored very poorly. Their average score was 5. This clearly shows that till the age of 12 students were enjoying their life and loving themselves. As soon as the biological changes start taking place, they start doubting on self, confused about future, start loving others and ultimately ruin their future.

A genius child is converted into an average and small adult within 18 years.

I just want to ask all the students of this age group – how could you judge yourself today and declare the final result which is yet to come! This is prejudice. Don't you remember that all greats and successful people were average and small like you when they were 14-15 years. Don't make any prejudgment for your life. Never say to yourself that as I didn't do well in school, I would never do well in my life. Never make your average/ failing picture images in your sub conscious mind. All research proves, there is no direct relation between your school achievements and life achievements.

Mahatma Gandhi, Einstein, Bill Gates, Ford, Ray Kroc, Oberoi, Abraham Lincoln, Ambani and many.... believed in self and the Law of Abundance. What about you? Are you still doubtful about yourself? Set a dream and challenge yourself! And start chanting "I LUV MYSELF" all the time, within. Entire universal power will come to help you to realise your dream.

LAW OF ASSOCIATION

Law of association is a natural law and has tremendous importance during studenthood. As I always tell students that as soon as hormonal changes start taking place in you, you should feel proud and happy that God is kind enough to you that your process of becoming male/female started. You should thank God with a deep breath. This process will take 5-6 years. During this period many changes will happen within you. So, you should

be very careful in selecting all your associates and friends. You should work like CSO – Chief Selection Officer. Theses six years are foundation years and your associates are going to play a very important role in making or breaking your dreams and your life.

During my I LUV MYSELF workshops, I always ask students – how many minutes you chat with your friends? I am usually surprised to know that today's students are investing rather wasting their valuable time and parent's money on internet/mobile in chatting @ 5-6 hours daily; that means 180 hours in a month and 2160 hours and around Rs. 1 lakh in a year. I would like to caution you that excessive use of internet / mobile can increase social isolation as well as lead to depression and many mental disorders.

Now you yourself evaluate whether your association is profitable or unprofitable! Friends, you are professional students and professional means, who knows his/her profession. You are also getting salary as your school fee and many other benefits from your parents. I have learned in my 25 years of professional career that if you are not generating profits, you are generating losses. And with losses, you can't survive. So, think about your association. It is rightly said that "your friends in life are like buttons on an elevator. They will either take you UP or take you DOWN."

This law says – be friendly to all but very selective in making friends. Save your time and money and invest the saved wealth in yourself to acquire skills and style. This is possible when you often chant "I luv myself" within and feel BIG in front of your eyes.

LAW OF COMMUNICATION

This natural law says that during the age of 12-18 years, your communication with self is most important for realising your dreams. I always demonstrate the example of mobile in my I LUV MYSELF workshops. Knowing a mobile number can't guarantee that you would get this number connected immediately after dialing. Out of five times, four times you hear "Line is busy, dial after some time". Isn't it! This is because of congestion in route. The same thing happens with your communication to you and to your God too.

Consciously you have made your dream to become a doctor. But you have forgotten to verbalise, visualise and emotionalise your dream of becoming a doctor. Thus, you have not created your picture image of a doctor who is wearing apron and sitting in his/her chamber and examining patients through re-programming processes suggested in this book. You can't become a doctor because you are distracted by your old average / failing picture images, you have created unknowingly about yourself in your subconscious mind. So, when you say that I am going to be a doctor without changing the picture images means your line is also busy like mobile because of distracting picture images of your subconscious mind. So, you are not able to communicate to yourself and to your God. Your God means your super conscious mind. Friends, you know that upper compartment of your mind is conscious and the last compartment is super conscious mind. Between these two compartments, subconscious mind exists

and this is a large data bank. What you decide consciously, knowingly or unknowingly, gets registered in your mind in three dimensional way.

So, I am cautioning you to remain alert and attentive during 12-18 years, while communicating with yourself and others. What you talk to yourself and repeat in your conscious mind all the time, you will become the same.

LAW OF TITHING

What you give, you will get. The more you give, the more you get. This is a natural law and very important during studenthood. Giving does't mean giving money only. A smile, a flower, a good wish, your old books, your old shoes and cloths, your time...... Your money comes last in law of tithing.

Instead of chatting on internet/mobile and wasting time and money, start giving something daily, weekly, monthly to those who are in need and see what you are getting! You will not believe, this habit of giving will change your entire perceptions and you will starts receiving.

I have observed in my workshops that students are not using this natural law. They are giving but slang and abusive languages, hate, deceit, fraud, tobaccos, alcohol, drugs and arms. And ultimately they are receiving heartaches, hospitalisation and jail. If you don't have to give anything then praise and bless everything around you. When you are praising someone or something, you are giving love and the more you praise, the more love you are giving and thus in return you will receive love in many fold. Praising

and blessing create positive aura around you and dissolves all negativity.

LAW OF LEMONADE

This natural law is also called the law of harvesting. You have to give something to yourself during the foundation years in acquiring skills, knowledge and style to become a star. You are a lemon. During 12-18 years, do something, add some skills, groom yourself and convert yourself in lemonade. You will become sellable. You have to create your own niche. And this takes time. Start playing the game of life and explore yourself.

Pepsi is selling NIMBOZ in Rs. 15/- by adding something from outside in few drops of NIMBOO, i. e. lemon of few paise. Now, Nimboz is a product of more than 20 crore. You can too become a product of crores, if you start chanting "I luv myself" within all the time and start adding something in you.

Always remember that what is inside will come out after squeezing. If you assume yourself as lemon, when squeezed, only juice of lemon will come out. So is with you. If you have love, kindness, respect, self control, serenity, joy, forgiveness, only those winning and wonderful qualities will appear in your style. if any negativity comes out in your style that means still you don't luv yourself and you are not converted yet into a lemonade.

LAW OF KARNI & BHARNI

This is also called as law of cause and effect. What you are receiving today is the *Bharani* (Outcome) of your *Karani* (activities) of the

past. If you are not happy with your *Bharani*, you have to change the *Karani* by taking 100% responsibility of all your activities from today and this is under your control.

LAW OF BELIEF

This is very important natural law during studenthood. What you believe of yourself, you will become the same. Beliefs are the most powerful force for bringing or creating changes in your life.

I am poor. I can't do this or that. These all are your limiting beliefs. And, this effects your performance. I can't speak in public seminars. I can't quit smoking or drinking alcohol. I can't become rich. These all are beliefs made by you only. And the beauty of mind is that what you believe good or bad, positive or negative, life or death, you will realise it.

During studenthood, your belief system gets affected by TV, Internet and Mobile because what you see, you believe. You know that your eyes influences your mind @87% and thus TV, Internet and Mobile create false perception which leads to false beliefs which ultimately ruins your life.

LAW OF CONCENTRATION

This natural law says that what you think all the time and concentrate on that thought, you will realise that thought because thoughts are things. On an average 60,000 thoughts enter into our mind during 24 hours. This law says that you have to focus on one thought, rest 59999 thoughts will automatically disappear. You have to concentrate on one single thought and this thought will

create your destiny. The decision to choose that single thought is under your control. Keep on thinking about that single thought all the time with feelings and activity will start automatically.

Suppose you want to become a Doctor, then think all the time how will you look when you become a Doctor. Create an image of Doctor in your conscious mind, though you are not a Doctor today. You have to create first a picture image in your conscious mind that you have become a Doctor and this image will get registered in your subconscious mind that is your GINN. The more you concentrate on your created image, the sooner and faster you realise that image in to reality. You always be alert while concentrating because your mind can hold only one thought at a time, either positive or negative. If you find that you are concentrating on negative thought and travelled to a fearful or a phobic proportion, you immediately stop thinking. Take deep breathes and change your movement. If you have been thinking about the negative thought while sitting, get up and start jumping. Replace that negative thought with a positive one. You will start feeling good.

LAW OF RESPONSIBILITY

This natural law says that you first decide to accept the responsibility and you will be in a position to control your life. As for example, driver of a bus or car, pilot of an aeroplane, driver of a train own the entire responsibility for whatever results his actions bring about. He realises fully that failure to correctly operate the above mentioned machines he controls can bring death to everyone on board. The same way your mind is a

thinking machine and failure to think correctly or positive will bring frustration, disappointments and failure in your day to day life and, for this you are responsible only. So, during studenthood you need to be responsible for your thinking, feeling and doing.

LAW OF ATTRACTION

This natural law is the most powerful law. This law says that you are the most powerful magnet in this universe. Your magnetic power is emitted through your thoughts.

This law says that positive attracts positive, negative attracts negative and like attracts like. So, as you think a thought, you will attract all like thoughts. This law is experienced in every moment by you in your life. Have you ever thought why, you get depressed or feel angry. This is because one thought of unhappiness, anger, anxiousness entered into your mind and unknowingly or knowingly you accepted this thought and as soon as you repeated this feeling of unhappiness, anger and disappointment in your mind, your mind starts attracting all unhappiness, anger and disappointments which are roaming and floating in this universe on the same frequency and make you unhappy, frustrated and depressed. You also experience this law of attraction while you entertain positive parts like listening to music, thinking about good time spent with your family and friends.

All above mentioned laws are natural and will work only when you are in harmony with yourself and you will bring harmony only when you start loving yourself. And for that you have to chant all the time I LUV MYSELF.

Who are you & where are you going?

My father often said to me when I was in std. 10th, "Son, you always ask yourself, who are you and where you are going." Now, after 30 years I realised the importance of these questions in life. I have been reading and hearing the word SPIRITUALITY very often since my childhood. But never tried to know the real meaning. I started feeling a change in my attitude towards myself after 7th June'05 when I met with adversity and lost everything. After this day I often asked this question to myself, "Who am I and where am I going?" This enquiry about me helped me to bring a paradigm shift in my attitude, behaviour and performance in my day to day activities. This enquiry about me helped me to understand the word SPIRITUALITY a bit.

As far as I know about SPIRITUALITY, this doesn't mean right or wrong; SPIRITUALITY doesn't mean from any angle about God; SPIRITUALITY has nothing to do about visiting pilgrimages in search of God; SPIRITUALITY is about knowing "who you are and where are you going?" This means exploring your limits, ultimate limit. This exploration starts from the age 5-6 only. As far as I know every human being is spiritual. Basically, we are spiritual animal. Everybody is striving for happiness and freedom. This simply means all are exploring themselves to know who they are, but unconsciously. 87-90% people are striving unconsciously.

If you want to go to meet your friend who is residing your next door and if you know the geography of the place, it would be very simple to reach there. But, if you don't know the geography, you can go around the world to search your friend's house and still get there. It may take 10 minutes, 10 years or 50 years. But, still you can find that house. So, my experience about spirituality confirms that everybody is on path and searching that SPIRIT, i.e GOD, who is within you. Majority are going around the world and some are just going straight WITHIN. This is the difference.

Fundamentally, this search or exploration to find you is within you. All the experiences are within you. It is you who is travelling and moving here and there searching you. It is you who talk about heaven or hell, God or devil, positive or negative. So, the basic thing is YOU, not somebody else. That's why I always say to students to search yourself within during 12-18 years and it can be possible only when you focus on yourself, when you love yourself. The earlier you understand this wonderful fact, the easier your life exploring journey would become and you would explore your ultimate limit, ultimate potential that is invisible.

Lord Buddha , Mahatma Gandhi, Mother Teresa, Nelson Mandela, APJ Abdul Kalam, Barak Obama, Sachin Tendulkar, Amitabh Bachchan, Amir Khan, AR Rahman, Bill Gates, Nitish Kumar, Manmohan Singh, Swami Ramdev, Sri Sri Ravishanker, Atal Bihari Vajpayee, Kapil Dev and many who explored their limits and many are busy in exploring their ultimate limits within.

What are you doing? You too are empowered for this exciting exploration that is YOU.

Abraham Lincoln's letter to the Headmaster of the school in which his son was studying........

" .... He will have to learn. I know that all men are not just, all men are not true.

- Teach my son that for every scoundrel there is a hero; that for every selfish politician, there is a dedicated leader.
- Teach my son that for every enemy there is a friend. It will take time, I know, but teach him if you can, that a dollar earn is of far more value than five found.
- Teach my son to learn to use and also to enjoy winning. Steer him away from envy if you can, teach him the secret of quiet laughter. Let him learn early that bullies are the earliest to lick.
- Teach my son if you can, the wonder of books but also give him quite some time to ponder the eternal mystery of birds in the sky, bees in the sun, and flowers on the green hill side.
- In school teach him that it is far more honourable to fail than to cheat.
- Teach my son to have faith in his own ideas, even if everyone tells him they are wrong.
- Teach my son to be gentle with gentle people and tough with tough. Try to give him the strength not to follow the crowd when everyone is getting on the band wagon.

- Teach my son to listen to all men but teach him also to filter all he hears on a screen of truth and take only the good that comes through.
- Teach my son if you can, how to laugh when he is sad. Teach him there is no shame in tears.
- Teach my son to scoff at cynics and beware of too much sweetness.
- Teach my son to sell his brawn and brain to the highest bidders, but never to put price tag on his heart and soul.
- Teach my son to close his ears to the howling mob and to stand up and fight if he thinks he is right.
- Teach my son gently, but don't cuddle fine steel. Let him have the courage to be impatient; let him have the patience to be brave.
- Teach my son always to have sublime faith in mankind.

This is a big order, but see what you can do. He is such a fine little fellow, my son."

If

You

Want

To

Succeed,

Speed up

FAILING!

But fail forward.

SUCCESS

I have missed more than 9000 shots in my career.

I have lost almost 300 games. On 26 occasions,

I have been entrusted to take the game-winning shot and missed.

I have failed over and over again in my life and that is the way I

succeed.

– Michael Jordan

There is nothing wrong in failing or making mistakes. Mistakes and Failures are part of life and essential for growth and success. But, you should not commit the same mistake twice. This shows a complete lack of self awareness. You are not an animal but Human being with SPARK. You can analyse what you are doing, right or wrong; A dog, a bird or even a monkey can't do this analysis.

- Amitabh Bachchan was rejected in his first audition test.
- Dhiru Bhai Ambani couldn't pass high school even. Moreover, he failed in his first venture.
- Albert Einstein couldn't speak until he was four years young. He couldn't read until he was seven. Moreover, he was not good in mathematics in his school.
- Thomas Edison was a stupid and he would never accomplish anything in his life, declared by his teacher when he was in school.
- Isaac Newton finished next to the lowest in his class and failed in geometry.
- Bill Gates failed in his class when he was fourteen years young.

WHAT IS SUCCESS!

To laugh often and much;
To win the respect of intelligent people
and the affection of children;
To earn the appreciation of honest critics
and endure the betrayal of false friends;
To appreciate beauty;
To find the best in others;
To leave the world a bit better, whether by
a healthy child, a garden patch
or a redeemed social condition;
To know even one life has breathed
easier because you have lived;
this is to have SUCCEEDED.
—Ralph Waldo Emerson.

FRIENDSHIP

Your friends in life are like **buttons** on an elevator.

They will either take you

UP

Or take you

DOWN

(So, be very selective in choosing your friends)

Internal Impact

and

Most important

FACTORS

YOU and the PRESENT MOMENT YOU HAVE!

Think

You are going to live on an average 70 years. Out of 70 years, you sleep around 35 years. So, you have only 35 years in hand for conscious living. If you are 15 years old, you have only 20 years left for conscious living. During this short period, you have to explore your potential. THINK & FEEL this important statistics. Don't waste time in loving others; start loving yourself. Things and circumstances will start unfolding on its own.

YOU

YOU

YOU

YOU

Are

The most important factor!

There will never be a better you than **YOU**. You are unique. You are special. The moment you start believing this important fact, you will stop competing with others but with yourself. Always think and plan, what will you do with you today. Because there will never be a better time to be the best **YOU** than today.

RIGHT ATTITUDE

Live in the present moment, not in future.

Do your best today, don't look for tomorrow.

– Sri Sri Paramahansa yogananda

ATTITUDE

The longer I live, the more I realise the impact of ATTITUDE on life. ATTITUDE to me is more important than facts. It is more important than the fast, than education, than money, than circumstances, than failures, than successes, than what other people think or do. It is more important than appearance, giftedness or skill. It will make or break an individual, a home, a society or a country. The remarkable thing is we have a choice every day regarding the attitude we will embrace for that day. We can't change the past. We can't change the fact that people will act in a certain way. We can't change the inevitable. The only thing we can do is play on the one string we have and that is our ATTITUDE. I am convinced that life is 10% what happens to me and 90% how I react to it and so it is with you. We are in charge of our ATTITUDE.

—Charles Swindoll

THINK

One day Lord Buddha was sitting near a pond.
He saw a little sparrow,
busy in bathing and flying somewhere.
He was watching her repeated activities of
bathing and flying. He could not resist himself. He asked,
"O little sparrow, what are you doing?"
Sparrow replied, "Are you blind? Don't you see,
I am trying to douse the fire which is blazing
the house of a poor farmer!"
Buddha asked, "Will you be able to douse the fire
with a few drops of water,
you are carrying in your wings?"
The little bird smiled and replied,
"I don't know whether I could douse the fire or not.
However, I am doing my best on my part.
When history will be written,
my name would appear in the list of fire dousers."

What are you doing?

HUMILITY

Humility comes from realising that **God** is the doer, not you. When you feel that, how can you be proud of any accomplishment? Think constantly that whatever work you are performing is being done by

the Lord through you.

– Sri Sri Paramahansa Yogananda

WILL POWER

Strengthen your will power, so that you will not be

controlled by circumstances,

but will **control** them.

SURRENDER TO GOD

No matter how hard you work, never go to bed without giving God the deepest attention. You would not die but die for God if it is necessary.

– Sri Sri Paramahansa Yogananada

Be wherever you like, do whatever you choose,

just remember that all what you do is known to ME.

I am the Inner Ruler of all and seated in your hearts.

I am the controller – the wire-puller of the show of this universe.

I am the Creator, Preserver and Destroyer.

Nothing will harm him,

who turns his attention towards ME.

– Words of Lord Sri Sai Baba.

Don't plan to surrender to your God,

when you will reach the age of 60. He will not accept you.

He may send you to hospital or jail.

Right age to surrender to God is between 12-18 years.

Because, during this age you are the most beautiful,

handsome, pure and innocent.

-MANUKUL

One day Mahatma Gandhi *returned late in the night*
after attending several public meetings and was tired.
As soon as he went to his bed, he fell in a deep sleep.
At around 2'o clock in the early morning,
he got up and started crying.
His disciples were astonished and
frightened and asked, "What happened, Bapu?"
Mahatma kept on crying and replied,
"Without remembering my Ram,
how could I sleep? I can't forgive myself.
How could I forget my Ram?"
He kept on weeping like a child and started chanting –
Raghupati Raghav Raja Ram, Patit Pawan Sita Ram.

Taa Kahun Prabhu Kuchh agam nahin, Ja par Tum anukul!
Tav prabhav barvanlahi jaari sakai khalu tuul!!
– Goswami Tulsidas

CONNECTION WITH SELF

Take a deep breath and connect with yourself in

every 15 minutes. Say THANKS to your

God, who is within.

You will never feel alone.

FEEL THE GOD WITHIN!

Forming a friendship with GOD is the very best way to cope with loneliness. With HIM as your friend, you never feel alone!

—Romans 8 : 38, 39 ; Hebrews 13 : 5,6.

TRUST

I heard a beautiful story of a little boy and his father in my childhood from my father. A little boy and his father were crossing a flimsy bridge. Father asked his little son, "Ravi, hold my hand so that you don't fall in to river." And, Ravi said," No papa. You hold my hand." Why? asked the puzzled father. "Papa, if I hold your hand and something happens to me chances are that I may let your hand go. But, if you hold my hand, I know for sure that no matter what happens, you will never let my hand go," Ravi replied.

Are you trust worthy? YES / NO.

STRESS

Is

An Ignorant state,

It believes that everything is **emergency.**

– Natalie Goldberg

Everybody including your loved ones, will often create panic as if you are going to lose everything, next moment and Your life is going to meet an end. This is a false perception. Suppose, you failed in your examination. Everybody will start blowing alarming whistle to you. Many will say , "you are finished". This false perception that something wrong will happen tomorrow is the main cause of STRESS. This is simply an ignorant state. Nobody on this earth knows what will happen tomorrow. Every problem is a lesson and it requires review only. You shouldn't get trapped in negative momentum, as up till now you are aware that your speed is 1000 mile per hour. Take three deep breathes and connect with your GOD within.

If you want to enjoy your studenthood and life

FOCUS

On

What is under your

CONTROL

And

Take actions!

One of the important facts I learned from my life is that SUCCESS is the result of a fine tune between making things happen and letting things happen. We can set our objective or dreams and realise our full potential by playing at our very best. We must do our part with a great sincerity and commitment and letting things unfold on its own. In other words, you can say

Do your job best, then let life do the rest.

Check your "I am restless" level

If you answer **"Yes"** to more than 2-3 Questions, you are stressed, anxious and restless.

- I have trouble concentrating when I study.
- I get extremely nervous about tests.
- I often have headache because of school/college.
- I have trouble sleeping before exams.
- I am concerned about what my friends think about me.
- I have trouble communicating with my parents and teachers.
- I worry a lot.
- I am pressurised by my parents to perform.

How to come out

From

Stress

Close your eyes. Take a deep breath. Start chanting

I LUV MYSELF

six times

Within.

Start activities Corresponding To Your DREAMS

Don't postpone things for tomorrow.

Don't watch TV more than one hour.

Don't listen to anything negative.

Do some jumping exercises, yoga,

dancing and listen to some good music.

Check your "I LUV MYSELF" Level

If your answer is "Yes" in more than 2-3 questions then you don't love yourself and you are suffering from poor self-image and you are leading towards failure:

- I don't love myself.
- I often doubt my abilities.
- I often think what could go wrong rather than what could go right.
- I often talk about my weaknesses.
- I find distrustful of others.
- I am easily intimidated by others.
- I always use slang language with my friends.
- I don't obey and respect my parents and teachers.
- I always bunk classes and tuitions.
- I always get up late in the morning.
- I always eat junk food.
- I used to surf internet and visit all adult/prohibited sites.

(Be honest while answering the above questions)

- I used to check out adult movies and magazines.
- I used to gossip/chat on mobile and internet hours and hours.
- I smoke and consume alcoholic drinks.
- I don't exercise or listen to good music.
- I watch TV more than one hour.
- I don't complete my homework/tuition work/project work in time.

How to improve your "I LUV MYSELF" level for better outcome of results from yourself:

- Practice verbalisation exercises daily (morning-evening).
- Practice visualisation exercise daily (morning-evening).
- Listen to instrumental music for 10 minutes in the evening and feel the music.
- Don't surf the internet without developing self-discipline.

(For verbalisation, visualisation and emotionalisation exercises, watch "I LUV MYSELF" CD)

Check your "I can" LEVEL

If your answer is "Yes" in more than 2-3 questions than you don't love yourself and you are suffering from failure attitude, you are leading towards failure:

- I always blame others for my problems.
- I have yet to commit to my dreams.
- I tend to dwell on mistakes.
- I feel tremendous pressure to perform.
- I have trouble sticking to my study schedule.
- I don't believe I am good.
- I take criticism personally.
- I always associate myself with negative people.
- I don't look for the best in others.
- I always roam and gossip.
- I don't mix up with people easily.
- I never say sorry or thank you to others.

Practice

YES, I CAN

Exercises

To develop

I CAN

Attitude.

(For YES, I CAN exercises, watch "I LUV MYSELF" CD)

Check your "I KNOW MYSELF" level

- When action needs to be taken, I take it myself.
- I learn from my mistakes instead of repeating.
- I like myself regardless of what others think about me.
- I expect the best from myself.
- I always laugh at myself.
- I am comfortable with myself, I know I am not perfect but who cares.
- I listen to what others are saying and wait for my turn to speak.
- I always love challenges in life.
- I always look for opportunities in every problem.
- I trust my intuitions and always enjoy feeling.
- I prefer to live in present.
- I help others without expecting any returns.

10-12 'YES'	:	YOU KNOW YOURSELF.
5-9 'YES'	:	You need to think about yourself.
2-4 'YES'	:	You are having deep-seated problems. Seek help. Start chanting "I Luv Myself" within all the time.

Six Common Questions

I came across while training and motivating students in my

"I LUV MYSELF"

Workshops across the country with

Answers/Advices

QUESTION 1.

I cannot concentrate while studying?

ANSWER AND ADVICE:

It is quite obvious and common in students of age group 12-18 years. This is because of hormonal changes which are taking place in your system. This is making you confused because you are observing many physical changes during this period. Moustache, beards are coming out; shoulders are getting broadened in boys. Likewise, breasts are getting enlarged and menstrual cycle starts in girls. You are getting noticed by opposite sex. Boys are producing testosterone, a male hormone. This is a creative hormone and initially makes you impulsive and restless. You start feeling attracted towards girls and you always want to be with them. This is further complicated if you are watching TV more than one hour and surfing internet and roaming, gossiping and chatting on mobile. Likewise, girls produce progesterone, a female creative hormone. This makes you beautiful and changes your physical appearance. Now you are not the same girl who used to be before these hormonal changes. You are also feeling attracted towards boys.

The above changes in you are the causes of losing focus and concentration in studies. However, these changes can make you more responsible and accountable too, if you start reprogramming your mind by loving yourself instead of declaring your love to somebody else. At 12, you just set your professional, personal, family and spiritual dreams and start verbalising, visualising and emotionalising all the time.

Start developing factors of stardom in you, which are defined in this book. This will take 365 days and within this time you will develop all the winning habits which will ultimately bring success in your life. By the age of 18, you will become a complete man and a woman. These years are very important and the foundation years of your life, so don't waste time, reprogram your conscious mind and fix your winning images in your subconscious mind.

If you are not enjoying your studies, take a deep breath, close your eyes and say six times with visualisation that "I am enjoying my studies". This is very simple.

Keep on practising and start enjoying your studies. I do practice all the time, too.

QUESTION 2

I USE TO STUDY VERY HARD BUT I COULD NOT GET MARKS IN MY EXAMS?

ANSWER AND ADVICE:

When you work hard, you are not enjoying. When you are not enjoying anything, you can't retain. So, you don't have to work hard while studying. You just start loving yourself and enjoying your studies. You will start getting all the things you want. Your marks are the outcome and results. If you are not happy with the results, you have to change your response and stop blaming your school, teacher, friends, parents and circumstances. This means you have to take total control of your day-to-day

activities and you will have to become a professional student. Professional means one who knows about his profession. As I am a professional trainer and to be successful as a trainer, I always give my 100% while training and the moment I start giving my 100%, I start enjoying and ultimately I start getting more in return. I start getting applause, appreciation, recognition, awards and experience, apart from my professional charges.

So, if you want to get all as a professional student, you just start giving your 100% as a student and take control of your activities. You will start receiving good marks, appreciation, trust of your parents and teachers and will receive awards. If you keep on doing good job all the time, you keep on getting more and ultimately achieve your dreams. And, this process starts when you start loving yourself as this is the mantra for success.

QUESTION 3

I always want the company of girls?

ANSWER AND ADVICE:

Please understand very clearly that if you are always willing to be with girls, you are leading to be in hospital or jail. You just take a deep breath and ask W7H from yourself, what you want in life? Every boy or girl wants the company of opposite sex during this age and it is not unnatural. But, I always say in my workshops to boys especially that if you want to love or marry Aishwarya, become Abhishek. This means, analyse and understand your strengths between 12-18 years. Stop wasting time in gossiping and

roaming with girls/friends. Start adding everyday the factors of stardom in you and create your own style. Verbalise, visualise and emotionalise your dreams and become a star in your chosen field like Abhishek. Aishwarya will come to you automatically and say "Will you marry me?"

So friends, please ask yourself very clearly in the age between 12-18 years, what you want in your life – girls or stardom. This is your choice. If you make fun in these years and waste time, your life will be very hard and miserable after 20.

QUESTION 4

I want to be a cricketer, singer, rock dancer, filmstar but my parents are putting pressure on me to become a doctor or an engineer?

ANSWER AND ADVICE:

Friends, your parents are not wrong all the time. To make you understand better, I would like to share one beautiful example. This occurred at one of my workshop. One 14 years, young boy came to me and started weeping. I asked "What happened to you?" He answered, "Sir, I am a very good dancer and want to be a film star like Akshay Kumar but my parents are not interested in my dreams. They always compel me to study hard, so that I could become an engineer and I am not interested in it". I listened to him very patiently. When he finished his dialogue, I asked him why don't you give a performance of Akshay kumar here as everything is ready to shoot your performance. Audience is also here to

clap for your good performance. Video camera is on and ready to shoot your performance. So, start acting and show everybody here that you are a born actor and prove your parents wrong.

He started thinking. He became silent and all his euphoria to become an actor vanished. I asked what happened! Come on. You are an actor. I am giving you an opportunity to perform. I will talk to your parents too, if you give a good performance here. Friends, he did't perform. He silently went back to his seat. Now, you all ask yourself, do you really want to become an actor, cricketer, singer, rock dancer? Be very clear first, then make a commitment with yourself. Start verbalising, visualising and emotionalising. Do something everyday to realise your dream. But the condition is that you don't compromise on your studies until you win the trust of your parents and teachers. You can't say that I don't want to become an engineer or a doctor for the sake of running away from studies. What do you think about Rahul Dravid, Anil Kumble, Srinath. They all are CRICKETERS and Doctors/Engineers, too. Don't blame your parents. If you want to become something, start demonstrating when opportunity comes to you. This will happen only when you start loving yourself.

QUESTION 5

Parents don't love me?

ANSWER AND ADVICE:

Start loving your parents. Don't expect anything in return.

QUESTION 6

I want to die. I am very short, fat, black, poor....?

ANSWER AND ADVICE:

Very Good. Again you are trying to do something which is against natural laws. You can't change many things here. You don't have the power to choose your parents, colour, country, religion, birth, etc. But, God has given you the power to change your circumstances and this power comes to you when you accept whole-heartedly your 'self' and start loving yourself. This mantra will connect with your God. Now, set your dreams after evaluating your strengths and tell Him about your dreams. Select a role model. Start developing factors of stardom. Always visualise your dream as if you have already achieved.

Friends, you are a lemon. Make yourself into lemonade and sell yourself to get success. For this you have to love yourself.

Start **Loving** Yourself

and

Start **Winning**!

Fixed Daily Activities of

a SUCCESSFUL Student

- Rise with the sun and complete your daily routine.
- Practice ILUV MYSELF excises for 15 minutes.
- Start for school/college/work with positive notes.
- Reach school /tuitions/office on time. Don't bunk.
- Eat healthy foods. Avoid junk food.
- Accomplish your all assignments today only. Don't postpone.
- Always think before you talk.
- Use and demonstrate positive body language always, even in adverse conditions.
- Always say within I LUV MYSELF and keep on thinking and visualising your dreams all the time .
- Be very selective in choosing friends.
- Be friendly with all.
- Love your parents, teachers and friends.
- Always talk to your parents, whenever you feel insecure.
- Talk to your God very frequently with the deep breath.
- Stop sleeping too much. Too much sleep makes genius students ordinary.
- Become an Idea Manufacturing Company (IMC) because one good idea can revolutionise your life and even the entire world.

ACTIVITIES OF A PROFESSIONAL & SUCCESSFUL STUDENT

- Be first in saying Hello or Namaste, when you meet another person.
- Always smile a lot because it is contagious and helps in creating a winning platform.
- Remember the first name of your friends and peers. This shows that you really care.
- When you are talking, look in the eyes. This shows you are confident and willing to talk.
- Become a good listener. Most of the people don't listen. When the other person has finished his talk then you start your side of talk.
- You always give sincere compliments. This will bring the best results.
- Love yourself.
- Believe in self.
- Believe in God.
- Always see good in others.
- See opportunity in every problem.
- Always focus on solutions.

- Always ready to give and contribute.
- Take 100% responsibility for your activities.
- Never blame others or make excuses.
- Have a dream for your life and keep the dream in sight.
- Love your parents and teachers.
- Laugh at yourself not at others.
- Have self discipline and control while watching TV and internet.
- Have a fix time to use mobile, not more than ½ an hour preferably in evening only.
- Have a fix schedule for your physical fitness.
- Always check your speed while walking and talking. (while walking add 25% and while talking subtract 25% in speed).

Failing and Suicidal Patterns in Students

Excessive and Goalless thinking

Negative Thinking

Worry

Compromised Activities

Poor Oxidation

Fear of Failure

Failure

Alcohol/Drugs

Fear of Dying

Suicidal Attempts

(This above mentioned pattern is because of your nagative momentum)

This pattern is very common and dangerous in this age group (12-18 years). 85% of school/college going students are aimless and goalless. They either don't have any dream or don't have any role model. Already they are receiving creative hormones, which is making them confused and restless. This is the time when self-discipline is required. Today's youth is busy partying, gossiping and chatting with their false friends on internet or mobile and creating all false and polluted images in their subconscious mind. Excessive thinking of anything leads to negative thinking and this negative thinking opens the door of failing and suicidal patterns unknowingly.

God has designed your mind in such a way that whatever you think repeatedly (Negative or Positive) and visualise and emotionalise the end result, it will help you to bring your visual pictures in reality. Your mind has nothing to do about your negative or positive results, loss or profits, failure or success and death or life. So, be very alert while you think. Any thought, if it is repeated 3-4 times in your conscious mind, will be accepted by your subconscious mind in three-dimensional format and your mind sensors start acting as antennas and start collecting the data from outside world to make you successful. If you are continuously thinking about failure, you will fail. But, if you are repeatedly thinking to succeed, you will be successful.

Successful life pattern

Goal focussed thinking

Repeated thinking

Goal focussed verbalisation

Goal achieved visualisation with emotions

Goal compulsive activities

Healthy Oxidation

Goal achievement

Health, Wealth and Prosperity

TOTAL SUCCESS

(This above mentioned pattern is because of your positive momentum)

TEN LESSONS FOR STUDENTS

Ten practical lessons that students don't learn in school. Our curriculum has created a generation of students with little concept of reality. They are set up for failure without a road map. Read the following statements slowly. Think, Feel and Do something ......

1. All is not well in life. Get used to it.
2. This world wouldn't care about your self esteem. You have to love yourself on your own.
3. You will not make Rs. 50,000/- per month right out of high school. You have to earn and it will take time.
4. If you think your teacher is good tough, please wait till you get a boss.
5. If you don't perform during your studenthood, it is not your parent's fault. So, don't make stories about your mistakes and failures. Learn from them.
6. Before you were born, your parents were not as boring as they are now. They became that way from paying your fees, cleaning your cloths and listening to your talks about how smart you are.
7. Your school may have done away with winners and losers but, life has not. In some schools, they have abolished failing grades.
8. Life is not divided into semesters. You don't get summer or winter off in your life.
9. TV is not real life. It creates false perception. Don't waste time on TV.
10. Mobile is the machine which creates confusion, tension and distraction. Don't get fascinated for this machine.

TEN CORE BELIEFS OF A SUCCESSFUL STUDENT

- Winning is a habit and so is Losing. The choice is yours.
- you are a winner or Loser, this depends on your THINKING you engage in.
- you are born to explore your true potential. You are empowered to create your own reality.
- your failures and adversities are your good times when you get some benefits.
- Nobody can defeat you or fail you until you accept defeat or failure and stop doing something or stop trying.
- you are born to excel in at least one area of your life.
- you are your own real enemy, when you put limitations on yourself, what you can do in your life.
- you can't achieve SUCCESS without great commitment.
- you can't achieve success on your own only. You need help of others too.

- you can't become BIG in front of others unless you become BIG infront of your own eyes. And this can be possible only when you start LUVING yourself.

THINK & FEEL the following statements:

- Everybody doesn't have to love me. I have to love myself.
- It is ok to make mistakes. All mistakes are lessons only in life.
- Other people are good and i am good too. All are potential to become successful.
- I don't have to control things. I have to connect only to get the right answer.
- I am responsible for my activities. I can't shift my responsibilities to others.
- I can handle all my problems and adverse situations with the help of my SAI/ GOD. God has given me MIND to analyse what is right or wrong for me.
- It is important to try because, knowing and not doing means not knowing.
- I am capable and I can do it. I have to just think differently all the time.
- I can change myself because change is very natural and it is only human being who can think, feel and change.
- Other people are capable and I don't need to change others but myself only.

Contribution from Students

1. Mirror

One day a bright child asked me
Where are you?
I replied that I am floating in Sea of Universe
Again he Questioned, "Who is your lover"?
I replied, "I love myself".
But he is finding me negative.
Because I am the special.
Because I have the power to control the Universe.
Because "I love you"!
But now "I love myself".
The child is no one
But the sprit of my success.
Because "I love myself".
as I am the mirror.

—Subhajit Dey
Class-IX
Jawahar Navodaya Vidalaya

2. My Mom

Kill the time, the time will kill you
My Mom always says this truth.

Slow and Steady wins the race
The only thing is to maintain the race

I hug my mom till she shout
Irritate her until she tell me to get out

Never praise the dish she cooks
But feel pleasure when she looks

I used to give her lot of worry
She smiles always when I am in hurry

Why I do this, I don't know
When I sweat she is like snow

All such events make me understand
This is Mom with whom I can ever stand.

I luv my mother

—Pratik Raj
X-A
Jawahar Navodaya Vidyalaya
Gandey, Giridih (JHARKHAND)

OM SAI RAM

Sabka Malik EK.

We are all One.

We are all connected and we are all part of the one energy or the one universal mind or the one consciousness or the one creative source. You call this one energy as OM, RAM, SHIV, KRISHNA, ALLAH, JESUS OR whatever you want to say. I call this one "OM SAI RAM".

You bring pain, frustration, disappointment, failure and poverty, when you are disconnected, separated from this one. This separation, this dis-connection is because of your negative thinking about yourself, your conditions and circumstances. This negativity comes when you lose "shraddha" i.e. "luv" in yourself and SAI. As soon as this shraddha, luv vanishes, you become inpatient, restless and this impatience and restlessness leads to poor oxidation. You start feeling breathlessness. This breathlessness is the first symptom which confirms that you are detached, separated and disconnected from one, i.e. SAI. So, to bring change in your condition, you have to do nothing but to "luv yourself". This "I LUV MYSELF" will connect you with one, i.e. SAI and you will start thinking, feeling, doing and succeeding in life.

This **One,** i.e. SAI, who has created this universe, is the supplier of everything and it is delivered through PEOPLE, CIRCUMSTANCES and EVENTS.

OM SAI RAM

ABOUT THE AUTHOR

RESUME

MANUKUL CHANDRA THAKUR

Preferred to be called as **"MANUKUL"**

29TH Sept, 1964	:	Came on earth to perform some specific assignment.
1980	:	Completed matriculation from N K High School, Gorea Kothi, Siwan, Bihar
1982	:	Completed 10+2 from UP inter college, Varanasi, UP
1984	:	Completed graduation in history from Rajendra College, Chapra, Bihar
1987	:	Completed post graduation from Bihar University, Muzaffarpur, Bihar. Started working as Medical Sales Representative at Jamshedpur in Systopic, a Delhi based Pharma Co.
1991	:	Got married and promotion in professional career as Area Manager.
1998	:	Joined TTK Pharma Ltd. as Regional Manager.
2001	:	Started a Pharma company with zero.
2001-03	:	As Managing Director and CEO of the company launched many innovational

		products and marketing modules successfully.
June, 2005	:	Met adversity when company was closed down on false rumours and severe financial loss.
2007	:	Relaunched the company but failed again.
2008	:	Cheated and ditched by many false friends and in the process lost all the parental and self earned properties.
Nov2008	:	Kicked out from in-laws' house by my brothers-in-law as lost all properties and business, thus became useless for them. After this incidence, started thinking seriously and put W7H to work and got the answer. I came to Delhi with my family and joined as CEO in a Cosmetic Co. I resigned from this company as I was not enjoying the job. I spent several days and nights without having single paise in my pocket. I always believed in myself and my SAI. I never bothered what people say about me. I kept on loving myself and things kept on unfolding automatically. I started training and motivating students, what I learnt from my life.
2009	:	My mother could not bear the losses and died on 15th Nov'09.

Conducted 100 "I LUV MYSELF" workshops across the country and trained more than 40,000 students, teachers and parents. Started writing "I LUV MYSELF", the mantra for success... An innovational mind-storming and self-exploring book for students, parents and teachers.

Feb'2010 : Completed manuscript of the book and talked to many publishers. SAI sent me to Pustak Mahal.

25th Feb'2010 : Founded *"I LUV MYSELF FOUNDATION"* – A non-governmental organisation, dedicated for exploring SAINESS among students for SUCCESS. Journey continued in the service of SAI.

Life is a mystery, I am exploring it!

I am now working on my next book "Why don't you become YOU?", "I Know Myself" and "Do you know, Papa!"

Afterword

I LUV MYSELF, the mantra for success... is an innovational mind-storming and self-exploring book for school and college students, teachers and parents for achieving success in studenthood and life by changing perception and belief.

I was really surprised when I interacted with around 60,000 school/college students, parents and teachers in my "I LUV MYSELF" workshops across India, and found that only 10% students, teachers and parents know about mind and subconscious power, perception, belief, factors of stardom, category of students, natural laws for students and how to reprogram the mind to achieve success. Moreover, 75-80% students in the age group of 12-18 years are negative and not enjoying their life. However, they are willing to improve themselves but do not know "how". In schools/colleges, teachers are busy in curriculum and academics. But, if majority of students are confused and restless, how can you teach them without changing their perception and belief! 10-12% students are totally out of place and out of track. *If they are not changing their own images immediately which they are holding in their subconscious mind, they are leading to jail or hospital. I am concerned about them.*

This book is written in such a manner that anyone can read and understand easily about his/her perception about himself. 365 days implementation programme for stardom is also given with required elaborations to bring the required change for success.

Please use this book as your activity book to bring required changes in your thinking, feeling and doing patterns.

Please help others too!

If you have been inspired by this book and want to help your friends, family members and others, please take one positive step today to bring a change in their life;

1. Gift "I LUV MYSELF" to your friends, family members and others. They will also learn the mantra for success and start enjoying their life.

2. Share your thoughts and feelings about this book with your friends and family members on facebook, Twitter or email.

3. If you are a Principal or parent, advise your students or wards to invest in this book so that everybody starts enjoying their life and in so doing, improve the atmosphere of school, society and ultimately this world.

You can mail your feedback to us at:

6thsensmail@gmail.com

Note: "I LUV MYSELF" book with CD is available at leading bookstores in India. If you want this book duly signed by Mr. Manukul, SMS your request with your full address on 09718206848.

"I LUV MYSELF"

Seminar / Workshop

For students, teachers, parents and professionals

I LUV MYSELF FOUNDATION in association with 6th sens Inc. invites all public and government schools / colleges to take advantage of Mr. Manukul's "I LUV MYSELF" seminars/ workshop for the development of 6th sense in their students, teachers, parents to bring a paradigm shift in their thinking, feeling and doing patterns in their day to day activities to achieve success.

His workshop will keep you mesmerised for months! Mr. Manukul has already trained more than 60,000 students through his life-changing workshop.

For workshop and seminar talk to

kanchan

09576553860

09718206848

This is an initiative of I LUV MYSELF FOUNDATION for children's education. For more details about Manukul and I LUV MYSELF FOUNDATION'S activities visit

www.iluvmyself.in

Praise for "I LUV MYSELF" workshop/seminar/book

I was restless and confused. I was not doing good in exams. I was not having any life's dream plan. But, after going through "I Luv Myseft" book written by Mr. Manukul, I scored very good in my 7th final exam and improved my grades in 8th class, too. I Love myself now. Thank You, Manukul Sir.

– Harshwardhan, Carmel Junior College, Jamshedpur.

"I Luv Myself" will improve the confidence of students and bring a change in their attitude, character and performance.

– The Prabhat Khabar, B. Deoghar Edition.

I am very happy to convey that the students of our vidyalaya are very fortunate to take part in the six hour "I LUV MYSELF" WORKSHOP of Mr. Manukul. It has a lasting effect on the mind of our students and teachers. I am confident that this workshop would bring a remarkable change in the attitude, behavior and performance of our students and teachers.

— Mr. BEGP Kumar, Principal, Jawaher Navodaya Vidyalaya, Durgapur, India.

Positive change in day to day activities of students and teachers has been noticed after the "I LUV MYSELF" workshop in our Vidyalaya.

— Mr. GSTomar, Principal, Jawaher Navodaya Vidyalaya, Shiekpura, Patna, India.

"I LUV MYSELF" will motivate students and bring a positive change in them.

— Sister Flavian, Principal , Carmel Jr. College, Jamshedpur, India.

"I LUV MYSELF" will help in exploring the true potential of a student.

— Dr. BKMishra, Principal, Delhi Public School, Birganj, Nepal.

"I LUV MYSELF" is a goldmine of commonsense i.e. sixth sense.

— Mr. Sanjay Prasad, Journalist, The Hindustan, Jamshedpur.

"I LUV MYSELF" is an amazing workshop. it is fascinating, full of information with fun. it is scientific, logical yet very simple. it touched my soul.

— Mr. PNJha, Regional Manager, Medley Pharmaceuticals Ltd, Jaipur, India.

I am not empowered but i am power. I am thrilled after attending "I LUV MYSELF" workshop..

— Mr. Sanjay Mishra, Editor, The Prabhat Khabar, Deoghar Edition, Jharkhand, India.

Moments of "I Luv Myself" workshops

Manukul

Parents meet

Parents meet at DAV School, Chaibasa

DBMS School, Jamshedpur

Delhi Public School,
Counseling Session

Navodaya Vidyalaya,
24 Paragana W B

Moments of "I Luv Myself" workshops

Kerala Samajam School,
Jamshedpur

Navodaya Vidyalaya
Darjeeling